Jesus Freaks

Stories of Those Who Stood for Jesus:

The Ultimate Jesus Freaks.

dc Talk
AND
THE VOICE OF THE MARTYRS

eagle

Eagle Publishing Ltd
Trowbridge, Wiltshire

JESUS FREAKS
STORIES OF THOSE WHO STOOD FOR JESUS
THE ULTIMATE JESUS FREAKS

© 2004, EAGLE PUBLISHING LTD,
6 KESTREL HOUSE, MILL STREET, TROWBRIDGE, WILTSHIRE BA14 8BE.

BRITISH LIBRARY CATALOGUING IN PUBLICATION DATA. A CATLOGUE RECORD FOR THIS BOOK IS AVAILABLE FROM THE BRITISH LIBRARY.

DESIGN BY THURBER, CREATIVE SERVICES, TULSA, OKLAHOMA.
PRINTED IN THE UK BY BOOKMARQUE.
ISBN 0 86347 584 1

Phil,

"Consider him who endured
from sinners such hostility
against himself so that you
may not grow weary
or faint hearted"

Hebrews 12:3

Never be ashamed of
Jesus,

Dedicated to...

**all those who
refused to
deny Jesus.
Your faith
was not in vain.**

Bible Class
2006

Jesus

People say

What will people
when they hear that
What will
when they find that
I don't really care
if they label
Cause there ain't

a stranger

That

What will
what will
I don't really care,
what else
There ain't no disguising

in a

Freak

think
I'm a **Jesus Freak?**
people do
    it's true?

me a **Jesus Freak**
no **disguising the truth.**

people think,
people do?

can I say,
the truth.

strange,
make me
best
friend
was born
manger?

Toby McKeehan & Mark Heimermann
Copyright ©1995 Fun Attic Music/ Achtober
    Songs/Up In The Mix Music
(All rights behalf of Achtober Songs and Up
    In The Mix Music administered by EMI
    Christian Music Publishing).
All Rights Reserved. International copyright
    secured. Used by permission.

A Message from Toby McKeehan

Galileo. DaVinci. William Shakespeare. Martin Luther. John the Baptist. These are the strange ones who challenged society with a different way of thinking. They were the rebels and heretics of their day. But if history is told correctly, no man has caused the worldwide stir that Jesus Christ did 2000 years ago. So many people today portray Jesus as weak, the out-of-date artifact hanging on a church wall or in a stained-glass window hoping for a brighter day. But Jesus was the non-conformist of all time. He took the conventions of religion, tradition, and love and turned them upside down. He faced the political and religious leaders of His day and spoke truths they had never heard before. He walked in our world as the human voice of God.

When I think of the boldest leaders and thinkers of our world, I believe Jesus stood above them all. He changed everything, and, by sacrificing His life, He changed the way I look at my fellow man. He is the one true reason I have a relationship with God. The more I learn about Him, the more I am drawn to Him and His ways. In a world that consists of fake lives and false promises, Jesus is authentic, and He died on the cross to prove it.

Real faith in Jesus seems to make people uncomfortable. Even in the open minded artistic world, lyrics about faith in Jesus can be considered offensive. I guess that's what the world calls a "Freak" — someone who commits to something wholeheartedly, without apology or compromise.

When our days on this planet are done, what will we be remembered for? That we had a nice car? That we made lots of money or became famous? Sometimes I have to struggle to keep my eyes set on the things of God rather than the things of man. But no matter how much I stumble, God's love is constant and it's His love that gives me the strength to stand up for Him.

For some, standing up for Jesus actually means dying for Him. In John 15:13 NIV Jesus says, "Greater love has no one than this, that he lay down his life for his friends." That's why we decided to title this book about martyrs *Jesus Freaks*. In its pages you will read story after story about those who would not compromise or apologize for their faith in Jesus Christ, even if it meant going to prison, being tortured, or facing death. These are the people who are changing our world by refusing to lay aside their relationship with Jesus for the mere sake of being accepted by the crowd. Such "Freaks" are the visionaries of our day.

My hope is that through their stories you will desire to know more about the man Jesus who has inspired such strength and courage for thousands of years.

A Message from Michael Tait

"What will people think?" That's the phrase that crept up on all of us when the album Jesus Freak *was coming together. That phrase crystallizes our fear of being different. Everyone has this need to be a part of something, to be included. The very nature of Jesus Freaks is to thrust away from the mob mentality, away from the things that society tells us to care about. And that can be scary. "What will people think if I'm different? What will they think if my opinion is weird? Who will like me if I stand out?" But every time I stand back and look at the bigger picture, I see a little of what God sees. I see the potential to make a difference. And I get the courage to break away from the crowd.*

When you open up this book you will learn about some of the biggest Jesus Freaks of all time: those who stood out from the crowd enough to be called martyrs. If Jesus was willing to give His life for me, and if these people, these martyrs, were willing to give up their lives for Him, how much does it take for me to truly dedicate my days on earth to Him?

Our mission may not involve hanging on a cross, being jailed, or being burned at the stake here in the West, but we have other, more invisible obstacles. Ours is a society built by pride, materialism, and dedication to the status quo. In a world built on free will instead of God's will, we must be the Freaks. While we may not be called to martyr our lives, we must martyr our way of life. We must put our selfish ways to death and march to a different beat. Then the world will see Jesus.

That's why I know the answer to my question, "What will people think?" They may think I'm weird. They may think I'm fascinating. But I don't really care. My life is God's. I've crossed the line from innocent bystander to hard-core participant in what Jesus has called me to.

What will people think? I hope, whatever I do, it makes them think of Jesus.

A Message From Kevin Max

The words "Jesus Freak" were first coined in the late sixties, when hippies became part of a new revival, the Jesus Movement. It was a time when music, poetry, and an open expression for Jesus Christ turned a new generation on to God. It merged rock and roll with the Gospel message, a wave we're still riding today known as contemporary Christian Music. It infused the Church with the arts. It shook up conventional worship. And, due to its "in your face" approach, it had a backlash. The rest of the world called these over-zealous young people "Jesus Freaks" as a derogatory term. But decades later a new generation is embracing that same passion for expression.

Being a Jesus Freak is having a passionate heart for Jesus, a willingness to extend that passion into all areas of life, be it poetry, music, art, or the hard choices made at life's crossroads. The lineage of Jesus Freaks actually extends much further back into history than the sixties. Many devoted followers through the centuries gave a new definition to the word "commitment" when they put their homes, their families, and even their lives on the line. Their love for Jesus was bigger than life itself. When I read their stories, I can't help but think of my own choices, my own commitments, and how much I owe to those courageous individuals.

Jesus Freaks are more than hippie kids and rock and roll. They are the dedicated followers of Jesus Christ who place His name above any other need or desire.

And as a Jesus Freak, I stand with thousands of martyrs around the world today who still face persecution because Jesus means more to them than their own lives or comfort.

A Message from Tom White,
Director of The Voice of the Martyrs

I met a man who stood up for Jesus in a meeting and was sent to prison for fourteen years. I just attended his ninetieth birthday party. He has scars on his neck and back, tortured by those who have never encountered the love of God. His name is Richard Wurmbrand. He speaks eleven languages and was a leader in the underground church in Romania. I suppose he might be the oldest Jesus Freak who is still living mentioned in this book.

If a Jesus Freak is someone who stands up or stands out when God calls, regardless of the circumstances, then Richard is your man. In 1947, this pastor taught Christians to walk backwards in the snow carrying Bibles into countries that forbid them. When border guards looked down from their towers in the morning, they ran with their police dogs in the wrong direction following the footsteps! When Russian soldiers invaded his homeland of Romania and there was great fear, Richard had his Christian group meet the Russians with Bibles in their language. God had brought a Russian "opportunity" to Romania. The Christians would give Bibles through the train windows to eager Russians before the KGB could stop them.

To be a Jesus Freak means you have to walk alone sometimes, not from doing something really weird, but because you strive to be a godly pilgrim — different from the values of this world. In prison, Richard made music with the chains on his arms and sang joyful praises to Emmanuel — the God with him.

The greatest pressure on the Freak who stands up for Jesus is the thought that they are alone — the only one. That is a lie. When I was on trial in Cuba for the Gospel, with a machine gun behind me, the prosecutor made fun of me. I told him about Hebrews 12:1, which mentions the cloud of witnesses around us. He was upset when I mentioned the saints and angels around me. Before trial I had been placed in special dark, cold cells with no furniture, no blanket, and no light. Cold air was blowing in above the door. Everything was taken from me. I began singing hymns and praise choruses. The guards got angry and pounded on the steel door with their fists. I was not destitute and alone. Second Corinthians 6:10 states that we can have nothing, yet possess everything. I fellowshipped with the Creator of everything.

The greatest encouragement I can give my fellow Jesus Freaks is that you are never alone. Those you will read about in this book are your family. They surround you.

Continue to set your light — Jesus Christ — on a hill.

mar·tyr (mär' ter) n. [< from the Greek word for "witness"]

1) One who chooses to suffer death rather than to deny Jesus Christ or His work.

2) One who bears testimony to the truth of what he has seen or heard or knows, as in a witness in a court of justice.

3) One who sacrifices something very important to further the kingdom of God.

4) One who endures severe or constant suffering for their Christian witness.

5) A Jesus Freak.

It is said that there are more Christian martyrs today than there were in 100 AD — in the days of the Roman Empire. According to the *World Christian Encyclopedia*, there were close to 164,000 Christians martyred around the world in 1999. An estimated 165,000 will be martyred in 2000.

Yes, in God

Yes, I Believe in God

She was 17 years old. He stood glaring at her, his weapon before her face.

"Do you believe in God?"

She paused. It was a life-or-death question. "Yes, I believe in God."

"Why?" asked her executioner. But he never gave her the chance to respond.

The teenage girl lay dead at his feet.

This scene could have happened in the Roman coliseum. It could have happened in the Middle Ages. And it could have happened in any number of countries around the world today. People are being imprisoned, tortured, and killed every day because they refuse to deny the name of Jesus.

This particular story, though, did not happen in ancient times, nor in Vietnam, Pakistan, or Romania. It happened at Columbine High School in Littleton, Colorado, on April 20, 1999.

Do you believe in Jesus?

Why?

He knelt praying in the middle of the night in a garden where He and His friends often went. He had told His friends, "Pray that you don't fall into temptation." His prayer was, "Father, if You are willing, let this cup pass from Me. But if this must happen, I will obey Your will." And then He prayed more earnestly. His sweat became as great drops of blood falling to the ground.

Soon soldiers came to take Him. He was betrayed by a best friend into their hands. The gospel of John tells us that the guards asked for "Jesus of Nazareth." When He answered, "I am He," they were knocked to the ground by the power of His confession. Peter, another friend, tried to rescue Him by attacking one of the high priest's servants and cutting off his ear. But Jesus rebuked Peter for his action, healed the servant's ear, and submitted Himself to the soldiers. He could have easily escaped, but He chose to be obedient to His Father's will.

He was taken before the high priest, where He was questioned and beaten. Then He was sent before the local governor to be tried. The priests demanded that He be crucified because He had declared He was God. He was questioned again, but the governor could find no guilt in Him. Still, the others called for His crucifixion. The governor sent Him out to be whipped, hoping to appease the priests.

The rest of the morning He was whipped and beaten beyond recognition. A robe was placed over His bleeding back, left until the lacerations dried to the cloth, and then it was ripped from His shoulders, reopening all of the wounds. Then they draped it over Him to begin the process again. They mocked Him as king of the Jews and made a crown of one-inch thorns, forcing it onto His head until the blood covered His face.

Again He was brought before the governor. This time he didn't ask the Pharisees and Sadducees, but he put it to the people, hoping they would show mercy on this innocent man. But the crowd called back, "Crucify Him! Crucify Him!" The governor washed his hands of the matter and turned Jesus of Nazareth over to the Roman guards for execution.

Jesus bore the weight of His own cross upon the torn flesh of His back and shoulders as He stumbled up the hill outside of the city. He was then nailed to that cross, raised up for all to see, and left there to die. The book of Matthew tells us He could have called twelve legions of angels to free Himself, but He didn't. He knew His sacrifice would pay the price for all mankind to be set free from sin and have the right to stand with God.

He was buried in a borrowed tomb, but didn't stay there long. On the third day He was resurrected from the dead, the keys of hell and death in His hands. He had paved the way for us to be born again, to become children of God, and to live forever with Him.

Immediately following His death, His friends and disciples were greatly afraid and hid. But after His resurrection, Jesus came and visited them, comforting and encouraging them. After He ascended to heaven, on the day of Pentecost, He gave them the Holy Spirit. A new boldness rose up within them. Jerusalem saw them convert three thousand on the first day. Then they spread to the corners of the earth to share the Gospel of Jesus Christ, no longer afraid. Every one of them except John was executed for proclaiming the name of Jesus. They never denied His name again.

Heroes. Brave men and women who lay down their lives for someone else.

The dying lieutenant turns to the young soldier for whom he has sacrificed his life. With his last breath he says, "Earn this."

The science officer exposes himself to excessive radiation to fix the ship, killing himself, but saving the lives of everyone else on board.

The oil driller on an asteroid headed for earth tears the air hose from the younger man's spacesuit, leaving him helpless and forcing him to stay behind on the shuttle. He then triggers the atomic bomb that splits the meteor, sacrificing his own life, but saving the world.

Our culture understands heroism. But we don't understand martyrs.

Most of the martyrs in this book could have saved their own lives if they had been willing to deny Jesus Christ. We wonder, "Why didn't they just say they weren't Christians and live?" or "Couldn't they just keep silent about their faith?"

Jesus said, "Greater love has no man than this, that a man lay his life down for his friends."

In ways that aren't always obvious, these martyrs — these Jesus Freaks — have heroically laid down their lives for us.

Why Did They Have to Die?

Standing before King Nebuchadnezzar, Shadrach, Meshach, and Abednego proclaimed, "We do not need to defend ourselves to you. If you throw us into the blazing furnace, the God we serve is able to save us from the furnace. He will save us from your power, O king. But even if God does not save us, we want you, O king, to know this: We will not serve your gods" (Daniel 3:16-18 NCV).

Live or die, they would not deny their faith.

In the last chapter of John, Jesus told Peter that he would die a martyr's death someday. When Peter saw John standing behind Jesus, he asked, "Master, what's going to happen to him?"

Jesus said, "If I want him to live until I come again, what's that to you? You — follow me." (John 21:22 THE MESSAGE.)

The purpose of this book is not to try to explain away the deaths of the martyrs, but to honour their conviction, commitment, and faith — and to build yours. Each of us must follow Jesus for ourselves. You may never have to face the decision of whether or not to die for your faith, but every day you face the decision of whether or not you will live for it.

What About the Persecutors?

Jesus said, "Love your enemies and pray for those who persecute you" (Matthew 5:44 NIV). On the cross He said, "Father, forgive them, for they do not know what they do" (Luke 23:34 NKJV).

As you read the stories in this book, you will also see a recurring theme: These men and women of God were more concerned with saving their torturers than their own lives. God has not called us to hate those who do evil, but to pray for them and bring them into His family as our brothers and sisters.

Seeing It God's Way

Some deaths seem senseless — but God sees things differently to us. As Tertullian, a Christian historian said, "The blood of the martyrs is the seed of the Church."

Some have been tortured because they refused to betray those who worked with them.

Some have stood firm, knowing that if they gave in — even a little — it would undermine the faith of many.

Some refused to be quiet because they realized their responsibility to tell the godless men around them of God's love so they too could be saved.

Some have simply been willing to lay down their lives for the One who laid down His life for them.

We shall not end our lives in the fire, but make a change for a better life.

Julius Palmer
Burned at the stake in England
1556

This is the end. For me, the beginning of life.

Dietrich Bonhoeffer
Hanged in Germany, 1945

For to me, living is for Christ, and dying is even better.

Paul the Apostle
Beheaded in Rome, AD 65

Heroic acts are often devastating, and there is a time for grief. But we must move on to discover the secret of the martyrs in this book. These believers were absolutely sure of eternal life. They were convinced that they were not ending their lives but exchanging their lives on earth for a life with their Lord in heaven.

Throughout history, many have died so you could experience the faith and freedoms you enjoy today.

You too can choose to stand strong. God will honour you and you will make a real difference in your world.

Learn about these martyrs.

Be encouraged by their heroic lives.

And make your life count!

Here are their

stories:

Remember the Lord's people
who are in jail and be concerned for them.
Don't forget those who are suffering,
but imagine that you are there
with them.

Hebrews 13:3 CEV

On Trial for Sharing the Gospel

Anila and Perveen
(these names have been changed to protect
the individuals and their families)
17 and 18 years old
Pakistan
1997

Anila met Perveen at school. As their friendship grew, Anila gave Perveen a Bible and taught her Christian songs. Perveen quickly learned Christian songs and began to teach them to her younger sister when her parents weren't home. Perveen's parents soon learned of the songs. Being strict Muslims, they were not happy about them. But rather than confronting Perveen right away, they got her younger sister to try to find out where she was getting this Christian influence.

Anila eventually invited Perveen to a Good Friday service. When the young Muslim heard the Gospel presentation, she immediately accepted Jesus. Perveen became very excited about her new relationship with Jesus and saw great changes take place in her life. She read her Bible and praised God boldly. Anila knew that, before long, her friend would encounter opposition from her family.

Perveen's parents were furious when they learned of her conversion. They had previously arranged for her to marry a Muslim man. When Perveen again refused, she ran away.

When Perveen's parents could not find her, they accused Anila and her pastor of kidnapping her. They had Anila arrested. Anila was slapped and beaten in front of her parents for over nine hours. Finally she was taken to prison.

Anila's pastor and his family were taken to prison on the following day. Anila and her pastor experienced horrible tortures in jail. She was whipped sixteen times (five times would make a normal man pass out). When they were released, Anila could not sit for two months, and her pastor could barely walk from the bruises on his hips and thighs.

Perveen was later found by her family. In Muslim nations, children are often severely beaten for converting to Christianity. Others are killed by their own parents or siblings for apostasy, converting to another faith.

To restore the honour of his family, Perveen's brother stabbed her to death. He then turned himself in to the local authorities. As is not uncommon in such situations, he was eventually released without incident.

Anila was then arrested on charges of kidnapping.

She was imprisoned, then released on bail a little more than a month later. She and her family went into hiding, as their lives were threatened by radical Muslims.

In May 1999, Anila was acquitted of all charges. Praise God for the prayers of faithful believers around the world! Continue to pray for her protection as she remains in hiding.

"I have seen the world," Anila said, "and it has nothing good. Jesus is my only peace."

There are hundreds, maybe thousands of other, similar stories that are never told of Christian children and teens being killed by their Muslim parents. Jesus said this would happen:

> **Brothers will give their own brothers to be killed, and fathers will give their own children to be killed. Children will fight against their own parents and have them put to death. All people will hate you because you follow me, but those people who keep their faith until the end will be saved.**
>
> Jesus
> (MATTHEW 10:21,22 NCV)

Pray for these young believers, that God will protect them and strengthen them. Pray for their parents, that they too will come to know Jesus as Lord. And most of all, forgive their persecutors and pray for the Muslim people to find the love of Jesus Christ and be saved.

Strengthened by Angels

Ivan Moiseyev
18 years old
U.S.S.R.
1970

Although he had never been there before, Private Ivan "Vanya" Moiseyev knew what awaited him at the Major's office. The Communists were endlessly calling him to head-quarters for talks, trying to "re-educate" him, to talk him out of his faith in God.

It was lunchtime. The sun was shining brightly in the blue sky and the snow was glistening. As Moiseyev walked along the snowy pavement, he praised God for this time alone, time to sing and pray.

The morning was so bright, at first Moiseyev didn't notice; suddenly, it caught his eye. A bright star began to fall from heaven. Like a comet, it came closer and became bigger and bigger.

He looked up to see an angel above him, bright and powerful. Moiseyev's heart was filled with joy — and fear.

The angel did not descend all the way to earth, but hovered about two hundred yards above the ground. He walked in the air above Moiseyev as though walking along the same road. Then the angel spoke:

"Ivan, go. Don't be afraid. I am with you."

Ivan couldn't speak, but his joy was like fire within him. Somehow he made it to Major Gidenko's office and knocked quietly at the door.

Major Gidenko, head of the Political Directive Committee, looked up as the young soldier entered. Ivan Moiseyev had been interrogated again and again by many others and had never backed away from his faith. Still, Gidenko was certain he could solve this problem.

"Moiseyev, you don't look like a poor pupil to me. Why are you not learning the correct answers?" he asked.

"Sometimes there is a difference between the correct answers and the true ones," Ivan answered. "Sometimes God does not permit me to give 'correct' answers."

"So, God talks to you? Who is this God of yours?" As soon as he had asked the question, Gidenko regretted it. Ivan leaned forward in his chair, his face glowing with joy at the opportunity to share his faith.

"Sir, He is the One who created all the universe. He greatly loves man, and sent His Son...."

Gidenko interrupted. "Yes, yes, I know the Christian teaching. But what has that got to do with being a soldier? Do you disagree with the teaching of the glorious Red army?"

"No, sir."

"But you do not accept the principles of scientific atheism upon which is based our entire Soviet state and the military power of the army?"

"I cannot accept what I know to be untrue. Everything else I can gladly accept."

"Moiseyev, no one can prove the existence of God. Even priests and pastors agree on that."

"Sir, they may speak about not being able to *prove* God, but there is no question about *knowing* Him. He is with me now, in this room. Before I came here, He sent an angel to encourage me."

Gidenko stared intently at Ivan. At last he spoke wearily, "I am sorry, Moiseyev, that you will not be reasonable. Your persistence will do nothing for you except bring discomfort. However, through the years I have found that men like you often come to their senses with a little discipline.

"I am ordering you to stand in the street tonight after taps are played. You will stand there until you are willing to reconsider this nonsense about talking Gods and angels.

"Since the temperature is likely to be thirteen degrees below zero, for your sake, I hope you quickly agree to behave sensibly. Tomorrow we shall make a plan together for your political re-education. You are dismissed."

Gidenko expected Moiseyev to hesitate, to reconsider. Instead, he squared his shoulders and walked quietly to the door.

"Private Moiseyev!"

When the soldier turned around, Gidenko noticed he was a little pale. Then he had understood the order!

"You will obey my instructions in summer uniform. That is all."

That night, as the bugle sounded, Ivan made his way down the stairs of the barracks and into the snowy street. He recoiled from the icy blast of wind that burned his ears and made his eyes water. His thin, summer uniform was no help in the bitter cold. He glanced at his watch. It was one minute after ten o'clock.

Tonight, he would have a long time to pray! But for the first time since he had been in the Soviet army, prayer did not come easily. He was worried. Could he stand out here all night? What if he froze to death? Would they let him freeze to death? What if he got so cold he gave in to their demands?

The "what ifs" flooded his mind and left it spinning. He knew he had to think of something else. Then he remembered the angel who had visited him that morning. The angel had said, "Do not be afraid, I am with you!" Suddenly he realized the angel's words had been for tonight! Although he could no longer see him, Moiseyev knew the angel was still there with him. He began to pray fervently.

It was twelve-thirty when he was distracted from his prayers by the crunching of snow. Bundled in their overcoats, hats, and boots, three officers were slowly making their way toward him.

"Private Moiseyev, have you changed your mind yet? Are you ready to come in and get warm?"

"No, comrade officers. As much as I want to come in and go to bed, I cannot. I will never agree to remain silent about God."

Even in the dim light Moiseyev could see the officers were amazed and confused. How could he stand such cold?

"Do you plan to stand out here all night long?"

"I don't see how anything else is possible, and God is helping me." Ivan checked his hands — they were cold, but not too cold. He could still move his toes easily. It was a miracle! He looked at the officers and could see that even in their coats they were already shaking from the cold. They were stamping their feet and slapping their hands, impatient to return to their heated barracks.

"You'll feel differently in another hour," the senior officer mumbled as they quickly turned away.

Ivan continued to pray for all the believers he knew. He sang Christmas carols. He prayed for every officer he knew and knew of. He cried out to God on behalf of the men in his barracks. But gradually his mind seemed to be floating somewhere outside of his head. As much as he tried, prayer eluded him.

Ivan was dozing on his feet when, at three o'clock, the senior officer on duty woke him and let him return to the barracks.

For the next twelve nights, Ivan continued to stand in the street outside his barracks. Miraculously, he did not freeze, nor did he beg for mercy. Ivan continued to speak about his faith to his comrades and officers. He sang about the glory of Jesus Christ in his barracks, though this was strictly prohibited. To those who threatened him, he replied, "A lark threatened with death for singing would still continue to sing. She cannot renounce her nature. Neither can we Christians."

Soldiers around him were converted, impressed by his ardent faith.

His commanders continued to interrogate him, trying to get him to deny Jesus. They put him in refrigerated cells. They clothed him in a special rubber suit, into which they pumped air until his chest was so compressed he scarcely could breathe.

At the age of 20, Ivan knew that the Communists would kill him. On July 11, 1972, he wrote to his parents, "You will not see me anymore." He then described a vision of angels and heaven which God had sent to strengthen him for the last trial.

A few days later, his body was returned to his family. It showed that he had been stabbed six times around the heart. He had wounds on his head and around the mouth. There were signs of beatings on the whole body. Then he had been drowned.

Colonel Malsin, his commander, said, "Moiseyev died with difficulty. He fought with death, but he died as a Christian."

The father of this Christian hero writes to us, "May it be that this living flower which gave the fragrance of its youth on the cross should be an example for all faithful youth. May they love Christ as our son has loved Him."

Letter from Vanya to his parents —
written June 15, 1972

"*My dear parents, the Lord has showed the way to me…and I have decided to follow it…. I will now have more severe and bigger battles than I have had till now. But I do not fear them. He goes before me. Do not grieve for me, my dear parents. It is because I love Jesus more than myself. I listen to Him, though my body does fear somewhat or does not wish to go through everything. I do this because I do not value my life as much as I value Him. And I will not await my own will, but I will follow as the Lord leads. He says, Go, and I go.*

"Do not become grieved if this is your son's last letter. Because I myself, when I see and hear visions, hear how angels speak and see, I am even amazed and cannot believe that Vanya, your son, talks with angels. He, Vanya, has also had sins and failings, but through sufferings the Lord has wiped them away. And he does not live as he wishes himself, but as the Lord wishes."

We continue to shout our praise even when we're hemmed in with troubles, because we know how troubles can develop passionate patience in us, and how that patience in turn forges the tempered steel of virtue, keeping us alert for whatever God will do next. In alert expectancy such as this, we're never left feeling short-changed. Quite the contrary — we can't round up enough containers to hold everything God generously pours into our lives through the Holy Spirit!

Paul the Apostle
Martyred in Rome, AD 65
(ROMANS 5:3-5 THE MESSAGE)

The First Jesus Freak

Stephen
Jerusalem, Israel
AD 34

Across the courtroom, the young man on trial continued preaching. The jury fidgeted nervously as he told of their religious heritage and forefathers. What did Abraham and Moses have to do with this Jesus? Another young man in the audience, about the same age as the defendant, seemed not to be listening. His mind was already made up on the matter of this Jesus follower. The crowd of Jewish leaders, however, grew more agitated at every word from the young defendant.

Suddenly the preacher turned to the audience. "You stubborn and hardheaded people! You're always fighting against the Holy Spirit, just like your ancestors did. They killed the prophets who told about the coming of the Righteous One. And now you have turned against Him and killed Him. You have received the law of God, but you have not kept it."

When the crowd heard this, they were even more furious, but the defendant ignored their growing anger. His face glowed like that of an angel, and he stopped talking and pointed to the ceiling. "Look! I see heaven open and the Son of Man standing at the right hand of God."

This was too much. Yelling at the top of their voices, they all rushed at him. They dragged him out of the city to stone him. He continued preaching all the way.

The young man who had been in the audience, one Saul of Tarsus, followed after them. He stood a short distance away from the defendant, looking steadily at the sky as the mob grew larger. The cries grew more heated now. A man handed Saul his coat, then stooped to pick up a stone as though waiting for a signal from Saul. Saul lowered his gaze, then looked directly into the man's eyes and nodded. It was time to silence the young preacher.

Stephen, the defendant, continued despite the crowd's jeers, because the Man he was telling them about was so important to him. He couldn't stop talking about Him. Several more men had now removed their coats, handed them to Saul, and began gathering rocks, many of them so large that the men had to lift them with two hands.

"This blasphemer must be dealt with!"

"He speaks against Moses!"

"We don't want to hear about your Jesus anymore!"

A rock sailed past Stephen's head. He stopped speaking long enough to duck it, dazed for a moment, then stood to continue. The second rock caught him near his temple, and he fell to his knees. Another hit his shoulder. Then there were too many to count.

"No more Jesus talk!"

"Let this be a lesson to all who would proclaim this Jesus!"

Another stone found its mark. Then another. He couldn't open his eyes for the sting of the blood. His clothes were torn by the blows and blood dripped freely from the tatters. He began to pray, "Lord Jesus, receive my spirit." Then he scanned the crowd until his eyes locked with those of the young man who held a bundle of coats. "And Lord," he continued, "do not hold this sin against them."

When he said those words, Stephen died.

Slowly men gathered their coats from young Saul, who was soon alone with the body of the young preacher. Saul had come to Jerusalem to help silence this growing craze about Jesus of Nazareth. Despite his hatred, he could not shake the young man's words and how fearlessly he had faced death. He stood staring at the body of the first martyr for this Jesus. The glow that had so angered Saul was still on the young man's face. He had seen it as the smug pride of a heretic, but could it have been something else? He quenched the thought and turned away, more determined than ever to crush this Jesus movement.

Saul did not persecute men like Stephen for much longer. One day soon after, on his way to Damascus to imprison more believers, he saw Jesus. From that encounter he later became Paul, the first Christian missionary, who travelled everywhere proclaiming the name of Jesus. He eventually wrote a good part of the New Testament.

It started with a seed placed in his heart by a young man full of faith, grace, and power — a Jesus Freak who could not stop telling people about Jesus, even if it meant his life.

I was in the central highlands in Vietnam when someone remarked about how the Christians suffer there. One Vietnamese Christian remarked, "Suffering is not the worst thing that can happen to us. Disobedience to God is the worst thing."

Tom White
Director of The Voice of the Martyrs
Imprisoned in Cuba for 17 months
for distributing Christian literature
1979-80

Walled In

Wrunken
Roneses, Flanders
1500s

"I found one!" The Inquisitor held up the forbidden book as he called to his assistant. "Bring in the mayor and his family. Someone is studying the Bible in this house!"

In the 16th century, Philip II sent the Duke of Alba to Flanders to stamp out the Protestants who insisted on reading the Scriptures in their own language. Anyone found studying the Bible was hanged, drowned, torn in pieces, or burned alive at the stake.

The Inquisitors had found the Bible while inspecting the house of the Mayor of Brugge. One by one, family members were questioned, but everyone claimed they knew nothing about how the Bible got to their house.

Finally the officials asked the young maid-servant, Wrunken, who boldly declared, "I am reading it!"

The mayor, knowing the penalty for studying the Bible, tried to defend her, saying, "Oh, no, she only owns it. She doesn't ever read from it."

But Wrunken chose not to be defended by a lie. "This book is mine. I am reading from it, and it is more precious to me than anything!"

She was sentenced to die by suffocation. A place would be hollowed in the city wall, she would be tied in it, and the opening would be bricked over.

On the day of her execution, as she stood by the wall, an official tried to get her to change her mind, saying, "So young and beautiful — and yet to die."

Wrunken replied, "My Saviour died for me. I will also die for Him."

As the bricks were laid higher and higher, she was warned again. "You will suffocate and die in here!"

"I will be with Jesus," she answered.

Finally, the wall was finished, except for the one brick that would cover her face. For the last time, the official tried to persuade her. "Repent — just say the word and you will go free."

But Wrunken refused, saying instead, "O Lord, forgive my murderers."

The brick was put in place. Many years later, her bones were removed from the wall and buried in the cemetery of Brugge.

Wrunken trusted her life to Jesus, knowing that the end of her life on earth was not the end of her life.

So we always have courage. We know that while we live in this body, we are away from the Lord. We live by what we believe, not by what we can see... We really want to be away from this body and be at home with the Lord.

Our only goal is to please God whether we live here or there.

Paul the Apostle
Martyred in Rome, AD 65
(2 CORINTHIANS 5:6-9 NCV)

Released From Death Row

Gul Masih
Pakistan
1992

The judge looked at Sajjad Husain, who was the only witness against the Christian Gul Masih. The judge liked what he saw: Sajjad was young and fervent, college-educated, and with his full beard he looked like a true Muslim.

No one else had heard the conversation between the two neighbours. No one could confirm that Masih had defamed the Islamic prophet, Mohammed. It was Sajjad Husain's word against Gul Masih's word.

The judge looked at Gul Masih. Despite constant persecution, Gul Masih had chosen to be a Jesus Freak. In fact, his name "Masih" means Messiah. Many Christians in Pakistan, especially those who convert to Christianity, unashamedly use this as a public source of identification with Jesus Christ.

Pakistan's blasphemy laws are harsh: Every critical word about Mohammed or the Koran, their holy book, is considered blasphemy, and violators are sentenced to death. (Twelve other Pakistani Christians have been accused in recent years under these laws. Five of them were acquitted by the courts, but then illegally murdered by Muslim extremists. Many others are still being accused.)

The judge nodded toward Husain and said, "I have no reason to disbelieve this witness."

Then he turned to Gul Masih. "I sentence you to death by hanging."

When news of Gul Masih's situation was published, Christians from all over the world wrote to him in jail to encourage him that people knew of his situation, that they cared, and that they were praying for him. He responded to a Canadian woman:

"First of all, I am thankful to you that you have encouraged me. My Lord has come to me twice in my prison cell. One day, I was sitting in my cell thinking about this injustice in a sad and hopeless mood. Suddenly the cell filled with light and my body trembled. I saw my Lord. Four days after this, my Jesus came again and overshadowed me by raising His hands and blessing me.

"From that day on, I have been happy and at peace. My Lord is with me in jail. He doesn't leave me alone.

"We are five members in our family. We have a great love for each other. I am very grateful to my Lord. He has fulfilled all my needs in the best possible way. I am also thankful to you and my other brothers and sisters who have supported me.

"I hope that by the grace of God we will see one another. Let us not forget the power of prayer."

In addition to writing to Gul Masih, many also wrote to the Pakistani Ambassador saying they were aware of the "unproven and unjust" sentences of Gul Masih and two other Pakistani Christians. One Christian leader says the law is used as a weapon against the Christians in the country. Many blasphemy charges are lies from a jealous, neighbouring shopkeeper or farmer.

These letters were used by God to help facilitate Gul Masih's release after almost three years in prison. In a miraculous turn of events, on November 29, 1994, the Lahore

High Court of Pakistan cleared Gul Masih of all charges of violating the blasphemy law and removed him from the danger of certain death.

Being released from death row does not exactly mean freedom for Gul Masih. His life remains threatened by Islamic fundamentalists who were outraged by the court's verdict. Within a month, the leader of the Muslim temple in Sarghoda issued a *fatwah*, an order for Gul Masih's assassination. Wanted posters were placed throughout the city of Sarghoda, pleading for his execution. Death threats were called out on the loudspeaker from the tower of the local mosque.

Gul Masih remains fearful for his life and is in hiding despite his release from prison.

There will even come a time when anyone who kills you will think he's doing God a favor. They will do these things because they never really understood the Father. I've told you these things so that when the time comes and they start in on you, you'll be well-warned and ready for them.

Jesus
(JOHN 16:2-4 THE MESSAGE)

Praise God for Gul Masih's release! Pray for the release of others being held on false charges. Pray for their protection and provision as they are released from prison.

And pray that Blasphemy Law 295C will be removed from Pakistan's legal system.

You can write to encourage believers who are in prison for their faith. You can also write to their governments on their behalf.

Check the back of this book for more information on countries who need prayer, what you can pray for them, how to get updated information on martyrs around the world, and other ways you can help free the persecuted church.

"I Am a Soldier of Christ!"

Roy Pontoh
15 years old
Indonesia
1999

The teens could tell that the shouts and chanting were getting closer and closer. An older teen looked nervously at his friend. "The Muslims are coming. We'd better hide the kids," he said. Others, following his lead, helped the smaller children find hiding places in the buildings nearby. Then they hid themselves.

It was January and a crowd of mostly Christian children and teenagers had gathered for a Bible camp at the Station Field Complex of Pattimura University on the island of Ambon, Indonesia. When the camp was over, cars came to take the laughing, rejoicing children back to their homes. But there were not enough cars to hold the young people.

Mecky Sainyakit and three other Christian men had gone to Wakal village to try to rent additional transportation to take the rest home. But they had not yet come back.

What the kids waiting for rides home didn't know was that on their way to the village, the men were attacked by a Muslim mob, who pulled them from their car and out onto the road. Mecky and one of the other men were stabbed to death, and later their bodies were burned by the mob. The two other men escaped with their lives.

Before long, the mob reached the University. They found many of the teens and forced them to come out of hiding.

Roy Pontoh was forced from his hiding place and made to stand before the mob.

"Renounce your Jesus, or we will kill you!" they threatened.

Roy was terribly frightened. Though trembling, he answered, "I am a soldier of Christ!"

At this, one of the Muslim attackers swung a sword at his stomach. The sword hit the Bible Roy held, and ripped into it, knocking it out of his hand. The man's next swing sliced open Roy's stomach. His last word was "Jesus."

The mob dragged Roy's body out and threw it in a ditch. Four days later, his family found it. Even though they are wracked with grief, Roy's parents stand proud of their son, who stood strong in his faith to the end.

Whoever declares openly — speaking out freely — and confesses that he is My worshipper and acknowledges Me before men, the Son of man also will declare and confess and acknowledge him before the angels of God.

Jesus
(LUKE 12:8 AMP)

A Christian prisoner in Cuba was asked to sign a statement containing charges against fellow Christians that would lead to their arrest. He said:

"The chain keeps me from signing this."

The Communist officer protested, "But you are not in chains!"

"I am," said the Christian. "I am bound by the chain of witnesses who throughout the centuries gave their lives for Jesus Christ. I am a link in this chain. I will not break it."

Her Last Prayer

Girl
16 or 17 years old
Asia
1970s

The Communist soldiers had discovered their illegal Bible study.

As the pastor was reading from the Bible, men with guns suddenly broke into the home, terrorizing the believers who had gathered there to worship. The Communists shouted insults and threatened to kill the Christians. The leading officer pointed his gun at the pastor's head. "Hand me your Bible," he demanded.

Reluctantly, the pastor handed over his Bible, his prized possession. With a sneer on his face, the guard threw the Word of God on the floor at his feet.

He glared at the small congregation. "We will let you go," he growled, "but first, you must spit on this book of lies. Anyone who refuses will be shot." The believers had no choice but to obey the officer's order.

A soldier pointed his gun at one of the men. "You first."

The man slowly got up and knelt down by the Bible. Reluctantly, he spit on it, praying, "Father, please forgive me." He stood up and walked to the door. The soldiers stood back and allowed him to leave.

"Okay, you!" the soldier said, nudging a woman forward. In tears, she could barely do what the soldier demanded. She spat only a little, but it was enough. She too was allowed to leave.

Quietly, a young girl came forward. Overcome with love for her Lord, she knelt down and picked up the Bible. She wiped off the spit with her dress. "What have they done to Your Word? Please forgive them," she prayed.

The Communist soldier put his pistol to her head. Then he pulled the trigger.

Most of those facing persecution today could have escaped if they had denied their faith. The question is not whether we are persecuted, but whether we are willing to lay down our life for our faith in Jesus Christ.

"I Am the Way, the Truth, and the Life"

Zahid
Pakistan
circa 1986

"When you catch the infidels, beat them! Allah will be pleased," Zahid encouraged them. The crowd of young men, the youth group of his mosque, waved their sticks and iron bars and cheered in agreement. Zahid's arrogance and hatred swelled. He felt he was doing well as a young Muslim priest. His parents would be proud. He had rallied a rather large group for this outing and they were nearly ready to go. Within minutes they would be combing the streets of their village for Christians to ambush.

Zahid had a proud heritage in Pakistan. His father and older brother were Muslim priests. As expected, Zahid had followed in their footsteps. Shortly after he was assigned to his first mosque, his hatred for Christians began to show itself as he rallied his followers against them.

To Zahid, as to many Muslims, Christians are heretics and should be punished. His government is becoming more influenced by *Sharia* law in some provinces. *Sharia* law calls for the death of anyone found guilty of blasphemy against the prophet Mohammed or the Koran. To these Muslims, rejecting Mohammed's teachings by becoming a Christian is the highest form of blasphemy.

When their fervour peaked, Zahid led his group into the streets. It was not long before they found a group of young Christians to attack. As the mob descended upon them, the young boys ran, one of them dropping his Bible. One of Zahid's group stopped, picked up the Bible, and opened it to rip out its pages. Zahid had always told his followers to burn all the Bibles they collected, but this time Zahid felt strangely compelled to keep it and study it in order to expose its errors to the people of his mosque. He quickly snatched the book from the man, encouraged him to chase the fleeing Christians, and tucked the Bible into his shirt for later.

Zahid reported in his own words what became of keeping that Bible:

"I was reading the Bible, looking for contradictions I could use against the Christian faith. All of a sudden, a great light appeared in my room and I heard a voice call my name. The light was so bright, it lit the entire room.

"Then the voice asked, 'Zahid, why do you persecute Me?'

"I was scared. I didn't know what to do. I thought I was dreaming. I asked, 'Who are you?'

"I heard, 'I am the way, the truth, and the life.'

"For the next three nights the light and the voice returned. Finally, on the fourth night, I knelt down and I accepted Jesus as my Saviour."

Zahid's hatred was suddenly gone. All he wanted to do was share Jesus with everyone he knew. He went to his family members and those in the mosque and told them what had happened to him over the last four nights, but they didn't believe him. His family and friends turned against him. They called the authorities to have him arrested so he would leave them alone about this Jesus. According to Islamic teaching, Zahid was now considered an apostate, a traitor to Islam, a man who had turned from his faith and accepted stupid lies. Thus, he was a criminal.

Zahid was locked up in prison for two years. The guards repeatedly beat and tortured him. One time, they pulled out his fingernails in an attempt to break his faith. Another time, they tied him to the ceiling fan by his hair and left him to hang there.

"Although I suffered greatly at the hands of my Muslim captors, I held no bitterness towards them. I knew that just a few years before, I had been one of them. I too had hated Christians.

"During my trial, I was found guilty of blasphemy. According to the *Sharia* law, I was to be executed by hanging. They tried to force me to recant my faith in Jesus. They assured me that if I cooperated there would be no more beatings, no more humiliation. I could go free.

"But I could not deny Jesus. Mohammed had never visited me; Jesus had. I knew He was the truth. I just prayed for the guards, hoping that they would also come to know Jesus."

On the day Zahid was to be hanged, he was unafraid of death as they came to take him from his cell. Even as they took him to his execution and placed the noose around his neck, Zahid preached about Jesus to his guards and executioners. He wanted his last breaths on earth to be used in telling his countrymen that Jesus was "the way, the truth, and the life." Zahid stood ready to face his Saviour.

Suddenly, loud voices were heard in the outer room. Guards hurried in to tell Zahid's executioners that the court had unexpectedly issued an order to release Zahid, stating that there was not enough evidence to execute him. To this day, no one knows why Zahid was suddenly allowed to go free.

Zahid later changed his name to Lazarus, feeling that he too had been raised from death. He travelled in the villages around his home testifying of his narrow escape from death. Many of the Christians did not trust him at first. But soon they saw his sincerity and received him into their family. They now assist him as he travels from village to village preaching Jesus as "the way, the truth, and the life."

I live in a land ruled by the false teaching of Islam. My people are blinded, and I was chosen by God to be His voice. I count all that I have suffered nothing compared to the endless joy of knowing Jesus, the way, the truth, and the life.

Zahid

No Longer Doubting

Thomas
Jerusalem, Israel
AD 34

Thomas knocked on the door of the upper room with the secret knock. It was immediately opened. He stepped inside and shut the door behind him. He was suddenly surrounded by his friends who were all talking at once. It was impossible to understand any of them!

"Thomas! Thomas! What Mary Magdalene said was true. He is alive!"

"Thomas, we've seen Him."

Thomas waved his hands, "Shhhh! I can't listen to you all at once! Peter, what has happened?"

"Thomas, we saw Jesus. He stood right here in this room with us. He talked to us."

Thomas frowned. "Peter, we've all been under a lot of stress. We haven't really slept since Jesus died. You must be imagining things."

"All of us imagining the same thing at the same time? I tell you, we saw Him! He walked right through the locked door."

"He walked through the locked door?" Thomas asked.

Everyone nodded.

"That explains it. It was a ghost! You didn't see Jesus, you saw a ghost."

"Thomas, we know we saw the Master! He showed us the wounds in His hands and His side. Our hearts could feel it was really Him."

Mary spoke up, "Oh, Thomas, if you'd have been here you'd know it was Him."

Thomas shook his head. "Did any of you touch Him? No. Then you can't know whether or not it was just a ghost. Believe what you want. But unless I see the nail marks in His hands and put my finger where the nails were, and put my hand into His side, I will not believe it."

A week later, Thomas was gathered with the rest of the disciples in the house with the doors locked. Suddenly Jesus came and stood among them and said, "Peace to you!"

Jesus focused His attention on Thomas. "Take your finger and examine My hands. Take your hand and stick it in My side. Don't be unbelieving. Believe."

Thomas fell to his knees. He didn't have to touch the wounds. He knew it was Jesus. He cried out, "My Master! My God!"

Jesus smiled, "So, you believe because you've seen with your own eyes. Good! But better blessings are in store for those who believe without seeing."

Thomas never doubted Jesus again!

Later, when the disciples travelled throughout the known world to preach the Gospel, Thomas was chosen to go to India and North Africa. Although he dreaded living among these savage tribes, God strengthened him, and he was able to convert many in these countries.

Around AD 70, he went to Calamina, India, where the people worshipped an image of the sun. Through the power of God, Thomas destroyed the image and put a stop to their idolatry.

The sun god's priests were furious. They accused him before their king, who sentenced him to be tortured with red-hot metal plates and then thrown into a glowing furnace.

To the amazement of all, the fire did not hurt Thomas — he was still alive in the midst of the furnace! When the priests saw this, they were so angry, they threw spears and javelins into the furnace at him. One of the spears pierced his side. He fell there dead.

Real followers of God know Jesus. Though they may not have seen Him with their eyes, they have felt His power, love, and joy in their lives. He is the Living Word and is so real to them that they would never deny Him, no matter the cost.

Through thick and thin, keep your hearts
at attention, in adoration before Christ,
your Master. Be ready to speak up and tell
anyone who asks why you're living the
way you are.

Peter the Apostle
Martyred in Rome, AD 65
(1 PETER 3:14,15 THE MESSAGE)

"Employ Your Whole Power Upon Me!"

Probius
Roman Empire
circa AD 250

Probius was whipped until the blood flowed, then laden with chains and thrown into prison. A few days later, he was brought out and commanded to sacrifice to the heathen gods. He knew that he would be tortured and killed if he refused. Still he courageously said:

"I come better prepared than before, for what I have suffered has only strengthened me in my resolution. Employ your whole power upon me, and you shall find that neither you, nor the Emperor, nor the gods you serve, nor even the devil, who is your father, shall compel me to worship idols."

Probius was sent back to further tortures and eventual death by the sword.

You never know how much you really believe anything until its truth or falsehood becomes a matter of life and death to you.

C. S. Lewis

A Song for the Lord

John Denley
England
1555

One day, on the way to visit some friends, John Denley was stopped and searched by the authorities, who found his written confession of faith. Denley believed the Church was built upon the apostles and prophets, with Christ as its head, and that the present state church, the Church of England, was not part of this true Church. In his time, many of its teachings were not according to the Bible.

For this he was turned over to a local government official, who turned him over to the bishop for questioning. Denley would not back down from his statement of faith, so he was condemned to die and turned over to the sheriff.

Within six weeks, he was sent to the stake to be burned. When they lit the wood beneath him, Denley showed no fear. He cheerfully sang a psalm as the flames rose around him. One of his tormentors picked up a piece of wood and threw it at him, hitting him in the face. He hoped to anger or silence Denley, but Denley only responded, "Truly, you have spoiled a good old song." Then he spread his arms again and continued singing until he died.

Jesus said that when we are mocked and persecuted because we are His followers that we can be happy about it:

*Be very glad! For a great reward awaits
you in heaven.*

Jesus
(MATTHEW 5:12 NLT)

We Were With Christ

Richard Wurmbrand
Romania
1945

One by one, the priests and pastors of Romania stood and offered words of praise for Communism and declared their loyalty to the new regime. Their statements of unity, propaganda for the Communists, were broadcast to the world over the radio, direct from the Parliament building.

It was a year after the Communists had seized power in Romania. The government had invited all religious leaders to attend a congress at the Parliament building — over 4,000 attended. First, they chose Joseph Stalin as honourary president of the congress. Then the speeches began. It was absurd and horrible. Communism was dedicated to the destruction of religion, as had already been shown in Russia. Yet bishops and pastors arose and declared that Communism and Christianity were fundamentally the same and could coexist. Out of fear, these men of God were filling the air with flattery and lies.

It was as if they spat in Jesus Christ's face.

Sabina Wurmbrand could stand it no longer. She whispered to her husband, "Richard, stand up and wash away this shame from the face of Christ."

Richard knew what would happen: "If I speak, you will lose your husband."

Sabina replied, "I do not wish to have a coward for a husband."

Pastor Wurmbrand took the stage. To everyone's surprise, he began to preach. Immediately, a great silence fell on the hall.

"Delegates, it is our duty not to praise earthly powers that come and go, but to glorify God the Creator and Christ the Saviour, who died for us on the cross."

A Communist official jumped to his feet. This would not do! The whole country was hearing the message of Christ proclaimed from the rostrum of the Communist Parliament. "Your right to speak is withdrawn!" he shouted.

Wurmbrand ignored him and went on. The atmosphere began to change. The audience began to applaud. He was saying what they had all wanted to say, but were afraid to.

The official bellowed, "Cut that microphone!" The crowd shouted him down. "The Pastor, the Pastor, the Pastor!" they chanted. The shouting and clapping went on long after the microphone wires were severed and Wurmbrand had stepped down. The Congress was ended for the day.

After this, Richard Wurmbrand was a marked man.

On Sunday, February 29, 1948, Pastor Wurmbrand was on his way to church when he was kidnapped by a small group of secret police. He tells what happened next:

"I was led to a prison thirty feet beneath the earth where I was kept in solitary confinement. For years, I was kept alone in a cell. Never did I see sun, moon, stars, flowers. Never did I see a man except the interrogators who beat and tortured me. Never did I have a book, never a bit of paper. When after many years I had to write again, I could not even remember how to write a capital D.

"To make the feeling of isolation worse, the prison was kept completely silent. Even the guards had cloth shoes so their steps could not be heard.

"When we were first put in solitary confinement, it was like dying. Every one of us lived again his past sins and his neglects of duties. We all had an unimaginable pain in our hearts thinking that we had not done our utmost for the Highest, for the One who has given His life for us on the Cross.

"I was in the depths of this remorse and pain, when suddenly, the wall of the jail began to shine like diamonds. I have seen many beautiful things, but never have I seen the beauties which I have seen in the dark cell beneath the earth. Never have I heard such beautiful music as on that day.

"The King of kings, Jesus, was with us. We saw His understanding, loving eyes. He wiped our tears away. He sent us words of love and words of forgiveness. We knew that everything which had been evil in our lives had passed away, had been forgotten by God. Now there came wonderful days; the bride was in the arms of the bridegroom — *we were with Christ*.

"We didn't know we were in prison. Sometimes when we were beaten and tortured, we were like St. Stephen, who while they threw stones at him, did not see his murderers, did not see the stones, but saw heaven open and Jesus standing at the right hand of the Father. In the same way, we didn't see the Communist torturers. We didn't see that we were in prison. We were surrounded by angels; we were with God.

"We no longer believed about God and Christ and angels because Bible verses said it. We didn't remember Bible verses anymore. We remembered about God because we experienced it. With great humility we can say with the apostles, 'What we have seen with our eyes, what we have heard with our ears, what we have touched with our own fingers, this we tell to you.'

"After years of solitary confinement, we were put together in huge cells, sometimes with 200 to 300 prisoners in each cell. I will not tell you the whole truth, because you could not bear to hear it. But this I will tell. Christian prisoners were beaten, then tied on crosses for four days and four nights without interruption. The Communists then stood around them, jeering and mocking, 'Look at your Christ, how beautiful He is, what fragrances He brings from heaven.' Then they kicked the other prisoners, forcing them to kneel down and to adore and worship this besmeared living crucifix.

"Then worse times came, the times of brainwashing. Anyone who has not passed through brainwashing can't understand what torture it is. From five in the morning until ten in the evening, seventeen hours a day, we had to sit perfectly straight. We were not allowed to lean or rest our head. To close our eyes was a crime. Seventeen hours a day we had to hear, "Communism is good, Communism is good, Communism is good. Christianity is stupid, Christianity is stupid, Christianity is stupid. Nobody believes in Christ anymore, nobody believes in Christ anymore. Give up, give up, give up!" For days, weeks, and years, we had to listen to this.

"Finally, the worst came. Communists torture those who believe in God. With red-hot iron pokers, with rubber truncheons, with sticks, with all kinds of methods, Christians were tortured by the Communists.

"And then the miracle happened. When it was at the worst, when we were tortured as never before, we began to love those who tortured us. Just as a flower, when you bruise it under your foot, rewards you with its perfume, the more we were mocked and tortured, the more we pitied and loved our torturers."

Many have asked Wurmbrand, "How can you love someone who is torturing you?" He replies:

"By looking at men...not as they are, but as they will be...I could also see in our persecutors a Saul of Tarsus — a future apostle Paul. Many officers of the secret police to whom we witnessed became Christians and were happy to later suffer in prison for having found our Christ. Although we were whipped, as Paul was, in our jailers we saw the potential of the jailer in Philippi who became a convert. We dreamed that soon they would ask, 'What must I do to be saved?'

"It was in prison that we found the hope of salvation for the Communists. It was there that we developed a sense of responsibility towards them. In Communist prisons the idea of a Christian mission to the Communists was born. We asked ourselves, 'What can we do to win these men to Christ?'

"The gates of heaven are not closed for the Communists. Neither is the light quenched for them. They can repent like everyone else. And we must call them to repentance. Only love can change the Communist and the terrorist."

When Pastor Wurmbrand was released in 1956, he resumed his work with the underground church. In 1959, he was turned over to the authorities again, this time by

one of his own co-workers. He was released the second time in 1964, and again resumed his work.

In 1965, friends paid the Romanian government a ransom of $10,000 so the Wurmbrand family could leave the country. They travelled to Scandinavia and England before settling in the U.S.

In May of that year, Richard testified in Washington, DC, before the Senate Internal Security Subcommittee, stripping to his waist and revealing eighteen deep torture wounds.

In 1967, the Wurmbrands formally started their mission to the Communists, Jesus to the Communist World. Today, this ministry is known as The Voice of the Martyrs and is still dedicated to serving the persecuted church wherever it may be found.

In 1991-2, we saw the collapse of Communism in the Soviet Union and Eastern Europe, and with it went the government-endorsed persecution of Christians. In retrospect, it is easy to see that the prayers and efforts of ministries such as The Voice of the Martyrs were key to the new freedoms the Gospel has found in these areas. Where not long ago, martyrs such as Richard and Sabina (who also spent three years in prison) were tortured for their faith, revival is breaking out. The Voice of the Martyrs continues its dedication to see the same freedoms won for the nations that continue to persecute Christians today.

It seems God is limited by our prayer life — that He can do nothing for humanity unless someone asks Him.

John Wesley
Founder of the
Methodist Movement

When a believing person prays, great things happen.

James, the Less
Thrown from the temple wall
AD 63
(JAMES 5:16 NCV)

You're familiar with the old written law, "Love your friend," and its unwritten companion, "Hate your enemy." I'm challenging that. I'm telling you to love your enemies. Let them bring out the best in you, not the worst.

When someone gives you a hard time, respond with the energies of prayer, for then you are working out of your true selves, your God-created selves. This is what God does. He gives his best...to everyone.

Jesus
(MATTHEW 5:43-45 THE MESSAGE)

"He Will Enable Me to Bear It"

Rose Allen Munt
England
1557

Rose Allen jumped from her bed and peeked out the window. There in front of her door stood a sheriff, two police officers, and a crowd of people carrying torches. They were talking with her father on the doorstep. She looked at the clock on the mantle. It was two in the morning.

Rose's mother, Alice Munt, had also been awakened by the loud pounding on the door. "What is it, Rose?" she whispered.

"They've come to get us, Mother," Rose whispered back. Rose could hear her father, William, letting the men in below. Then she heard footsteps coming up the stairs.

Friends had warned them of the danger of not attending the official church, but their sense of duty to the truth was stronger than their fears. They continued to worship in secret places with a few men and women of like faith. Now the authorities had come to take them away.

Alice, who was not in good health, was so shaken up by the sudden alarm that she felt faint. She asked the sheriff if her daughter could get her some water before they all left for prison.

The sheriff allowed Rose to go to the well. She took a candle and a pitcher to the well and returned with the water. As she came back towards the house, the sheriff met her at the door and said, "Persuade your father and mother to act more like good Christians and less like heretics. Then they'll soon be set free."

"Sir," Rose replied, "they have a better instructor than I, for the Holy Spirit teaches them — one who, I hope, will not allow them to err."

"Well! It's time to lock up such heretics as you!" the sheriff replied. "I reckon you will burn with the rest, for company's sake."

"No, sir," Rose replied, "not for company's sake, but for my Christ's sake, if I have to. And I trust in His mercies, that if He calls me to do it, He will enable me to bear it."

One of the sheriff's men shouted, "Prove her now, and you shall see what she will do by and by."

With that, the sheriff took the candle from the girl, and holding her wrist in a firm grip, put the lighted candle under her hand, burning it across the back for so long that the skin peeled off, the tendons cracked, and the bones showed.

"Cry, wench! Let me hear you cry!" he yelled.

Rose refused to utter a sound.

When he finally pushed her away, Rose said, "Sir, have you done what you will do?"

"Yes, and if you don't like it, then mend it."

"Mend it!" said Rose, "No, the Lord mend you, and give you repentance, if it be His will. And now, if you think it good, begin at the feet, and burn to the head also. For he that sent you to this work shall pay you your wages one day, I promise you."

Having said this, Rose carried the water into the house to her mother.

The same morning, the sheriff and his men also arrested six others. After they had been in prison a few days, they were all brought to trial. Each one answered with firmness and refused to change their belief in any way. They were sentenced to be burned at the stake.

When they were brought out, the martyrs knelt, said their prayers, and were tied to the stakes. When the fire rose all around them, they clapped their hands for joy in the fire.

The people who looked on — thousands of them — cried out, "Lord strengthen you! The Lord comfort you! The Lord pour out His mercies upon you!" and other words of comfort.

The martyrs gave themselves to the flames with such courage that all who saw them were amazed.

For centuries, godless torturers have been amazed that Jesus Freaks aren't afraid of them — even when threatened with death — but continue to respect, honour, and obey God.

Don't be bluffed into silence or insincerity by the threats of religious bullies. True, they can kill you, but then what can they do? There's nothing they can do to your soul, your core being. Save your fear for God, who holds your entire life — body and soul — in his hands.

Jesus
(LUKE 12:4,5 THE MESSAGE)

"I Will Go Straight to God"

Jack Vinson
Kiangsu Province, Mainland China
1931

The bandit told the missionary, "I'm going to kill you. Aren't you afraid?"

Jack Vinson replied simply, "Kill me, if you wish. I will go straight to God."

Jack Vinson's courage inspired his friend E. H. Hamilton to write this poem:

> Afraid? Of What?
> To feel the spirit's glad release?
> To pass from pain to perfect peace,
> The strife and strain of life to cease?
>> Afraid — of that?
>> Afraid? Of What?
> Afraid to see the Saviour's face
> To hear His welcome, and to trace
> The glory gleam from wounds of grace?
>> Afraid — of that?
>> Afraid? Of What?
> A flash, a crash, a pierced heart;
> Darkness, light, O Heaven's art!
> A wound of His a counterpart!

Afraid — of that?
Afraid? Of What?
To do by death what life could not —
Baptize with blood a stony plot,
Till souls shall blossom from the spot?
Afraid — of that?

"The Highest Words"

Nikolai Khamara
U.S.S.R.
1970s

"What kind of men are these?" wondered Nikolai Khamara. "They show joy while suffering. They sing in very dark hours. When they have a piece of bread, they share it with someone who has none. Morning and evening, they fold their hands and speak to someone whom no one can see. As they do, their faces shine."

For months, Khamara had watched the Christians who shared his cell in the Communist prison. Unlike the believers who were in prison for refusing to deny their faith in Jesus, Khamara was there for crimes he had committed. Arrested for robbery, he had been sentenced to prison for ten years. He described himself as "a man with no conscience."

One day, two of the Christians sat down with Khamara. He told them the sad story of his life and finished by saying, "I am a lost man."

One of the Christians asked Khamara, "Suppose somebody loses a gold ring. What is the value of that gold ring when it is lost?"

"What a foolish question!" Khamara replied. "A gold ring is a gold ring. You have lost it, but somebody else will have it."

"Then what is the value of a lost man?" the Christian asked. Answering his own question, he continued, "A lost man, even one who is a thief or an adulterer or a murderer, has the whole value of a man. He is of such value that the

Son of God forsook heaven for him and died on the cross to save him."

Khamara understood.

The Christian said to the robber, "God loves you. You are valuable to Him.

"When Jesus met drunkards, robbers, prostitutes, or others who had committed great sins, He never asked them what sins they had committed. Instead, He told them, 'Be of good cheer. Your sins are forgiven.' I also tell you, Khamara, that your sins are forgiven because Jesus died for you. You only have to believe."

Khamara became a Christian.

When he finished his prison term and was set free, he joined the underground church even though it was in constant threat from the KGB. He became a faithful member of his local congregation.

Some time later, the pastor of Khamara's church was arrested. The authorities beat and tortured him, hoping he would tell the names of the church members and give them information that would help them stop the printing of Gospel booklets that had been circulating throughout their province. He was tortured, but he told them nothing. If he had, thousands of his fellow believers would have been arrested.

After he had beaten the pastor repeatedly without success, the captain of the investigation said, "We will not torture you anymore. We have another method."

They arrested Nikolai Khamara. They brought him before the pastor and told him, "If you do not tell all the secrets of your church, we will torture Khamara in front of you."

The pastor could not endure someone suffering for him. He asked Khamara, "What should I do?"

Khamara said to him, "Be faithful to Jesus and do not betray Him. I am happy to suffer for the name of Christ."

The captain said, "We will gouge out Khamara's eyes." The torturers picked up a knife and started toward Khamara. The pastor could not bear it. He cried to Khamara, "How can I look at this? You will be blind!"

Khamara replied, "When my eyes are taken away from me, I will see more beauty than I see with these eyes. I will see the Saviour. You remain faithful to Christ to the end."

When he had finished, seeing that the pastor had not yet given them the information they wanted, the captain turned to the pastor again and said, "If you do not betray your church, we will cut out Khamara's tongue."

In despair, the pastor cried, "What should I do?"

Khamara's last words were, "Praise the Lord Jesus Christ. I have said the highest words that can be said. Now, if you wish, you can cut out my tongue."

Khamara died a martyr's death.

Let us run with endurance the race that God has set before us. We do this by keeping our eyes on Jesus, on whom our faith depends from start to finish. He was willing to die a shameful death on the cross because of the joy he knew would be his afterward. Now he is seated in

the place of highest honour beside God's throne in heaven. Think about all he endured when sinful people did such terrible things to him, so that you don't become weary and give up.

Hebrews 12:1-3 NLT

"My Life Is a Prayer"

Mary Khoury
17 years old
Damour, Lebanon
During the Lebanese civil war, 1975-1992

Mary Khoury and her family were forced to their knees before their home. The leader of the Muslim fanatics who had raided their village waved his pistol carelessly before their faces. His hatred for Christians burned in his eyes. "If you do not become a Muslim," he threatened, "you will be shot."

Mary knew Jesus had been given a similar choice, "Give up Your plan to save sinners, or You will be crucified." He chose the cross.

Mary's choice was similar. "I was baptized as a Christian, and His word came to me: 'Don't deny your faith.' I will obey Him. Go ahead and shoot." The report of a gun from behind her echoed in the valley and Mary's body fell limply to the ground.

Two days later, the Red Cross came into her village. Of all her family, Mary was the only one still alive. But the bullet had cut her spinal cord, leaving both her arms paralysed. They were stretched out from her body and bent at the elbows, reminiscent of Jesus at His crucifixion. She could do nothing with them.

More words from the Lord came to Mary. Even though she was now handicapped, she knew God had a plan for her life.

"Everyone has a vocation," she said. "I can never marry or do any physical work. So I will offer my life for Muslims, like the one who cut my father's throat, cursed my mother and stabbed her, and then tried to kill me. My life will be a prayer for them."

Such prayers shatter the governments of those who persecute Christians as billions of dollars spent on atomic bombs could never do. They also bring those who hate Christians face-to-face with the Son of God.

Mary's example encouraged others to take a heroic stand in Lebanon. Many died, were wounded, or fled the country during Lebanon's civil war. Some stayed, as did one missionary who was too concerned with his flock to flee to safety. Though the blast from a shell exploding in his home left him deaf in one ear and killed the family of five who lived next door to him, he was still strong in spirit. One ear was enough for him to use in spreading the Gospel. "People are coming to the Lord every day," he reported in 1990, one of the worst years of the war.

Dear friends, never avenge yourselves. Leave that to God. For it is written, "I will take vengeance; I will repay those who deserve it," says the Lord…

Don't let evil get the best of you, but conquer evil by doing good.

Paul the Apostle
Martyred in Rome, AD 65
(ROMANS 12:19,21 NLT)

Why I Came

Anne Askew
England
1546

Anne Askew was imprisoned and greatly tortured for her faith. Placed on a cruel rack, her joints and bones were pulled out of place. She fainted from the pain, but when she regained consciousness, she preached for two hours to her tormentors.

On the day of her execution, she was carried to the stake in a chair because her bones were dislocated and she couldn't walk. At the last moment, she was offered the king's pardon if she would recant. She said:

"I did not come here to deny my Lord and Master."

She died praying for her murderers in the midst of the flames.

If God is with us, no one can defeat us… Can anything separate us from the love Christ has for us? Can troubles or problems or sufferings or hunger or nakedness or danger or violent death?… In all these things we have full victory through God who showed his love for us.

Paul the Apostle
Martyred in Rome, AD 65
(ROMANS 8:31,35,37 NCV)

"A Pirate From
the House of Prayer"

Aida Skripnikova
19 years old
U.S.S.R.
1961

The young woman stood on the corner handing out small cards with poems on them. Some took them because they were interested in what she might be handing out, some because she was incredibly beautiful, but most probably took the cards because of the joy and love that showed in her smile as she looked each person in the eye and handed them a card. Each card contained a poem she had written herself. Each poem declared the love and joy she had from knowing Jesus as Lord and Saviour.

For this she was arrested and brought to trial. Before the court she boldly testified, "The society which you, the Communists, are building can never be just because you yourselves are unjust." She was sentenced to one year of imprisonment.

When she was released, she went straight back to her work for the underground church. Because of her beauty, determination, and boldness, she was labelled "a pirate from the house of prayer" by the Communist newspaper Izvestia.

One of the things she dared to write was, "You, the atheists, can meet together at any time and do whatever you like — talk, read, or sing. Why, then, can we not visit one another? What law forbids this? Why can we not pray or read the Bible whenever we want? We are allowed to speak about

God only in church. You would certainly not acquiesce if you were allowed to talk about the theatre only in a theatre or about books only in a library. *In the same way, we cannot be silent about what constitutes the whole meaning of our life — about Christ.*" Again she was arrested and this time was sentenced to four years in prison, but she did not waver.

By the age of 27, Aida was facing her fourth prison term, yet prison seemed to do little but increase her love for God's Word and its importance to her faith. "If it were the other way around, that we had a plentiful supply of Bibles and that there were none in England, I'd be prepared to be the first to take Bibles there.... In prison, the most difficult thing was to live without a Bible."

Once, a gospel of Mark was smuggled in to her. "When the guards learned that I had a gospel, they became alarmed and searched the whole camp. During the second search, they found it. I was punished for this and had to spend ten days and ten nights in solitary confinement in a cold cell. But two weeks later I was given a whole New Testament which I was able to keep almost until the day of my release.

"The prison was searched many times, but each time the Lord helped me. I knew in advance about the search and was able to keep the precious book. Many other prisoners helped me hide the book, even though they were not Christians."

The guards did many other things to try to discourage her and make her deny her faith, but some of these backfired on them. "Once the guard showed me a food parcel. He told me that it contained chocolate and other good things. It was not given to me, but it was an encouragement to know that my friends cared about me. That fact meant much more than the food. On another occasion, I was told ten packages had arrived for me from Norway, but I was not given these either... *It is a great joy for us to experience definite spiritual fellowship with Christians in different parts of the world. This gave us hope in prison.* I want to send an expression of love from us all to those who have cared about us and prayed for us."

When she was released from her fourth term, Aida had changed drastically. The movie-star beauty of her youth was not only gone, but at only thirty years of age she looked more than fifty. She was haggard and worn by the years of imprisonment. If you had seen her, you would never have recognized her as the same woman, except for one thing: her smile. It still reflected the love and joy of knowing Jesus as Lord and Saviour.

Of her last and hardest term in prison, Aida wrote, "One text became clearer than ever before, 'My yoke is easy, my burden is light' (Matthew 11:30). Jesus Himself spoke these words and during the three years of prison I came to understand how real and true they are."

In 1991, some twenty years after her fourth and final prison term, the Soviet Union broke up due to the fall of Communism. The government persecutions of Christians has stopped there, at least for a time. The faith and fight of Aida and the others in the underground were not in vain.

In 1992, couriers from The Voice of the Martyrs found Aida — sick, pale, and thin — living in a clean, neatly-kept apartment in a crumbling old building in St. Petersburg. She was an island of cleanliness and order in the midst of chaos; a picture of her heart and spirit. It was clear to see that she held no bitterness for her former torturers, only forgiveness. She was surprised about the attention her story had drawn from around the world, but was extremely grateful for it. She said, "I have only been able to endure because of the many prayers from around the world. Otherwise I would not have persevered."

Don't forget about those in prison. Suffer with them as though you were there yourself. Share the sorrow of those being mistreated, as though you feel their pain in your own bodies.

Hebrews 13:3 NLT

Preaching From the Rooftop

James, the Less
Jerusalem, Israel
AD 63

James looked down from where he stood, balanced carefully at the highest point of the temple in Jerusalem. Far below, he could see that the streets were filled with people. It was Passover, and Jews from all over the known world had come to the Holy City.

A hand grabbed his arm, pulling him off balance. "Get on with it!" a voice threatened. Behind him, a safe distance from the dangerous ledge, stood the chief priest, scribes, and Pharisees. "Deny that Jesus of Nazareth is the Messiah! Before all these people, deny that Jesus was the Son of God and that He was resurrected from the dead," they demanded.

James the Less was one of the twelve disciples chosen by Jesus. He was also one of Jesus' younger brothers, as was Jude. He had obviously known Jesus and walked with Him for many years. He had seen Jesus alive again after His crucifixion and resurrection.

James risked another glance at the street below. Many of the people down there knew him. For thirty years, he had been the bishop of the church at Jerusalem. During that time, he wrote a book of the Bible, the Epistle of James. He had openly preached Jesus as the Messiah and the resurrected Son of God on almost every street corner. How could he deny what he had seen with his own eyes, heard with his own ears, and touched with his own hands: his risen Lord?

Through his preaching, his prayers, and his example, James converted many people to Christ. He was on his bare knees so often, worshipping God and praying for forgiveness for the sins of the people, that his knees became numb and calloused, like the knees of a camel. This also earned him the nickname of "James the Just." He was respected by everyone, even many who opposed what he taught and believed.

Feeling threatened by the rapid growth of the church, the chief priest, scribes, and Pharisees came up with a plan. They would force this well-known church leader to deny his faith before the multitude. But James refused to cooperate.

From his place at the top of the temple, he preached with more boldness than ever. Every person in the crowd below looked up as he proclaimed, "Jesus is the promised Messiah! He is sitting at the right hand of God, and shall come again in the clouds of heaven, to judge the quick and the dead!"

When the crowd below saw his courage and heard his bold words, they loudly praised God and magnified the name of Jesus. Enraged, two or three of the religious leaders jumped forward and pushed James off the temple roof.

Miraculously, James was not killed by the fall; only his legs were broken. Then the priests, scribes, and Pharisees said, "Let's stone the 'just man' James." They picked up rocks to stone him to death. James, kneeling on his broken legs, prayed, "Lord, forgive them, for they do not know what they are doing."

One of the priests, when he heard James praying, begged the others to stop, saying, "What are we doing? 'The Just' is praying for us. Stop the stoning! Stop the stoning!"

While he was shouting this, another man ran up with a big, heavy stick in his hand and struck James on the head. James died instantly from the blow, still in prayer.

The word "martyr" originally meant someone who tells what he has seen, an eyewitness. Jesus Freaks are people who have seen Jesus' power in their own lives and just can't help telling others about it. A favourite saying of a teenage girl who boldly approaches other teens is, "If you knew what I know about Jesus, I'd want you to tell me!"

We're not keeping this quiet, not on your life. Just like the psalmist who wrote, "I believed it, so I said it," we say what we believe. And what we believe is that the One who raised up the Master Jesus will just as certainly raise us up with you, alive. Every detail works to your advantage and to God's glory: more and more grace, more and more people, more and more praise!

Paul the Apostle
Martyred in Rome, AD 65
(2 CORINTHIANS 4:13-15 THE MESSAGE)

"We Have Your Nephew"

Peter
8 years old
Philippines
1992

"We have your nephew," said the handwritten note. "If you surrender to us, we will return the boy to his parents." Brother MT stared at the message. It was from the leaders of the New People's Army (NPA), the military arm of the Communist Party of the Philippines. People in many parts of the Philippines have been threatened and persecuted for years by this group of terrorists.

Brother MT is an evangelist in the Philippines. He travels regularly into the mountains to preach to the terrorist groups. Peter, his eight-year-old nephew, frequently went with Brother MT on his evangelistic trips. He was a special help to him in children's meetings in the mountain villages.

Because of pressure from the NPA, Brother MT was often forced into hiding. Still, as a result of his ministry, some of the NPA soldiers had given their lives to Jesus Christ and left the organization. MT had counted the cost and was prepared to give his life for the Gospel, but he was not prepared for this! He knew there was no hope that his surrender would save his nephew. He knew they would both be killed; still, he hesitated.

The boy's parents insisted that MT ignore this order and continue his evangelistic outreach. As a result, the parents gave their son for the Gospel. Peter was killed on Good Friday, April 17, 1992. He was tortured for three hours and suffered very much. His hands were tied with wire, and the terrorists struck him in the legs and head with an axe. Finally, he was beheaded.

The abductors have warned the boy's parents and MT that if they do not stop their ministry, they will return and torture them. Brother MT is continuing his dangerous work in the mountains among the terrorist groups.

A minister I had heard of in Romania had been horribly beaten and was thrown back into the cell with the other prisoners. He was half-dead, with blood streaming from his face and body. As some of the prisoners washed him, others cursed the Communists. Groaning, the minister said, "Please, don't curse them! Keep silent! I wish to pray for them."

Richard Wurmbrand
Spent 14 years in a
Communist prison
Romania
1940s, 50s, and 60s

"We Will Cut Off Your Feet!"

Milon G.
Bangladesh
1996

The angry crowd yelled after the lone bicyclist, "If we see you again, we will cut off your feet. Then see if you can ride your bike!"

This was not the first time Milon G. had been threatened by angry crowds of Muslims. But such threats have not quenched his zeal to take the truth of God's Word to his countrymen.

"I ride to the villages on my bicycle and carry Christian literature. In the rains, I hold an umbrella in one hand and steer with the other. I often fall down and get muddy and scratched. At night, I hold a flashlight. I sing from the Psalms when I ride. The Christians I meet do not have an extra blanket for me, so I try to make it back home to sleep."

Milon was a teenager when a friend gave him some gospel booklets. "I hid them in a steel trunk in my bedroom. At night I would get my key, open the trunk, and read with a kerosene lamp. Having studied in a Muslim fundamental school for twelve years, I had known about Jesus as mentioned in the Koran, but I didn't know Him as Saviour. I accepted Jesus in 1992 and was baptized secretly 400 kilometres from my home."

Ever since then, Milon has been persecuted by Muslims. "I sold clothing in the local market and began placing some Christian books in my shop for other Christians. When Muslim men learned of this, they would walk into my shop and just take shirts, pants, and socks from the shelf without paying for them. If I asked for money they threatened to beat me. Anytime someone is interested in the booklets, I give them one."

Milon says, "We are going through many problems, but still we have Jesus Christ. We have peace through Him, and we have the hope that when we die we will go to heaven."

We are confident of all this because of our great trust in God through Christ. It is not that we think we can do anything of lasting value by ourselves. Our only power and success come from God. He is the one who has enabled us to represent his new covenant.

Paul the Apostle
Martyred in Rome, AD 65
(2 CORINTHIANS 3:4-6 NLT)

The Thundering Legion

A Legion of Roman Soldiers
Sebaste, Armenia, Eastern Roman Empire
(now Sivas, Turkey)
Under Emperor Licinius, AD 320

The Roman governor stood resolutely before the forty Roman soldiers of the Thundering Legion. "I command you to make an offering to the Roman gods. If you will not, you will be stripped of your military status."

The forty soldiers all believed firmly in the Lord Jesus. They knew they must not deny Him or sacrifice to the Roman idols, no matter what the governor would do to them.

Camdidus spoke for the legion, "Nothing is dearer or of greater honour to us than Christ our God."

The governor then tried other tactics to get them to deny their faith. First he offered them money and imperial honours. Then he threatened them with torments and torture with the rack and with fire.

Camdidus replied, "You offer us money that remains behind and glory that fades away. You seek to make us friends of the Emperor, but alienate us from the true King. We desire one gift, the crown of righteousness. We are anxious for one glory, the glory of the heavenly kingdom. We love honours, those of heaven.

"You threaten fearful torments and call our godliness a crime, but you will not find us fainthearted or attached to this life or easily stricken with terror. For the love of God, we are prepared to endure any kind of torture."

The governor was enraged. Now he wanted them to die a slow, painful death. They were stripped naked and herded to the middle of a frozen lake. He set soldiers to guard them to prevent any from coming to shore and escaping.

The forty encouraged each other as though they were going to battle. "How many of our companions in arms fell on the battle front, showing themselves loyal to an earthly king? Is it possible for us to fail to sacrifice our lives in faithfulness to the true King? Let us not turn aside, O warriors, let us not turn our backs in flight from the devil." They spent the night courageously bearing their pain and rejoicing in the hope of soon being with the Lord.

To increase the torment of the Christians, baths of hot water were put around the lake. With these the governor hoped to weaken the firm resolve of the freezing men. He told them, "You may come ashore when you are ready to deny your faith." In the end, one of them did weaken, came off the ice, and got into a warm bath.

When one of the guards on the shore saw him desert, he himself took the place of the traitor. Surprising everyone with the suddenness of his conversion, he threw off his clothes, and ran to join the naked ones on the ice, crying out loudly, "I am a Christian."

Some call it "the mystery of martyrdom." Why would seeing 39 believers who were willing to die for their faith inspire a highly-trained soldier, in the prime of his life, to

join them in death? It seems so foreign to our western way of thinking. It is amazing to see how God works through these tragic situations to call more people to Himself.

Unless a grain of wheat is buried in the ground, dead to the world, it is never any more than a grain of wheat. But if it is buried, it sprouts and reproduces itself many times over. In the same way, anyone who holds on to life just as it is destroys that life. But if you let it go, reckless in your love, you'll have it forever, real and eternal.

If any of you want to serve me, then follow me.

Jesus
(JOHN 12:23-26 THE MESSAGE)

Suffering saints are living seed.

Charles Spurgeon
19th Century Theologian

"There Is Freedom Everywhere"

Maria and Varia
18 years old
U.S.S.R.
1960s

Maria asked through the iron bars, "Varia, don't you regret what you did?"

"No," she answered. "And if they would free me, I would do it again and would tell them about the great love of Jesus. Don't think that I suffer. I am very glad that the Lord loves me so much and gives me the joy to endure for His name."

This was the first time Maria had been able to visit Varia in prison. Her friend was thin, pale, and beaten, but her eyes shone with the peace of God and an unearthly joy. The two Russian teenagers had once been schoolmates in a Communist boarding school. Varia, a member of the Communist Youth Organization, had constantly teased and tormented Maria, a Christian. In response, Maria prayed for the young Communist with special concern.

One day Varia said, "I cannot understand what a being you are. Here so many insult and hurt you, and yet you love everyone."

Maria said, "God has taught us to love everyone, not only friends, but also enemies."

"Can you love me, too?" Varia asked.

Maria hugged her, and they both began to weep. Not long afterward, Varia received Jesus as her personal Saviour and witnessed openly to everyone about it.

Maria wrote to her parents, "We went together to the assembly of the godless [the school's Communist Youth Club meeting]. I warned her to be reserved, but it was useless. I went with her to see what would happen.

"After the Communist hymn, Varia came forward before the whole assembly. Courageously and with much feeling, she witnessed to those gathered about Jesus her Saviour. She implored all to give up the way of sin and to come to Christ.

"All became silent and no one interrupted her. When she finished speaking, she sang with her splendid voice the whole Christian hymn: 'I am not ashamed to proclaim the Christ who died to defend His commandments and the power of His cross.'

"Afterwards...afterwards they took Varia away. We know nothing about her. But God is powerful to save her. Pray!"

Months passed after their single visit in prison. Then Maria received a letter from her friend who was in a Siberian labour camp. Varia wrote:

> My heart praises and thanks God that, through you, He showed me the way to salvation. Now, being on this way, my life has a purpose and I know where to go and for whom I suffer. I feel the desire to tell and to witness to everybody about the great joy of salvation that I have in my heart. Who can separate us from the love of God in Christ? Nobody and nothing. Neither prison nor suffering. The sufferings that God sends us only strengthen us more and more in the faith in Him. My heart is so full that the grace of God overflows.
>
> At work, they curse and punish me, giving me extra work because I cannot be silent. I must tell everyone what

the Lord has done for me. He has made me a new being, a new creation, of me who was on the way of perdition. Can I be silent after this? No, never! As long as my lips can speak, I will witness to every one about His great love.

Here there are many who believe in Christ as their personal Saviour. More than half of the prisoners are believers. We have among us great singers and good preachers of the Gospel. In the evening, when we all gather after heavy work, how wonderful it is to pass at least some time together in prayer at the feet of our Saviour. With Christ there is freedom everywhere. I learned here many beautiful hymns and every day God gives me more and more of His Word.

All our brethren greet you and are glad that your faith in God is so powerful and that you praise Him in your sufferings unceasingly.

Yours,
Varia

Varia just couldn't keep quiet about what Jesus meant to her, just like the apostles, Peter and John, who were also threatened for speaking out about Jesus. Here's what they said:

Whether it's right in God's eyes to listen to you rather than to God, you decide. As for us, there's no question — we can't keep quiet about what we've seen and heard.

Acts 4:19,20 THE MESSAGE

The Power of Prayer

Orson Vila
Cuba
1995

At 9:00 A.M. on May 24, 1995, Cuban police surprised Pastor Orson Vila at his home and took him prisoner. The next day, thousands of believers filled the streets in front of the government offices in Camaguey, protesting the unjust arrest.

It was the latest move by Castro's government to implement a new law designed to close down house churches everywhere. Orson, who pastors a large house church with a congregation of 2,500, is also superintendent of the Central District of the Assemblies of God Church in Cuba.

During the previous four years, in an apparent opening up of religious freedom, the Communist government permitted the development of these house churches. But upon seeing the unstoppable growth of new believers, they changed their point of view.

The church in Cuba was in revival as never before. There were eighty-five new house churches in the area of Camaguey alone! The government leaders were furious, and proclaimed that these house churches "threatened" the Cuban government. They tried to force the leaders, like Orson Vila, to close all the house churches.

None of the churches were willing to close.

Despite the tremendous demonstration of support by believers, Orson was not given a fair trial. His lawyer had no opportunity to provide a defence. On May 24, he was sentenced to one year and nine months in prison.

Twenty-three years ago, Brother Orson gave up his medical career to dedicate himself full-time to preach the Gospel throughout Cuba. Since that time, he has been an evangelist, the leader of the Christian youth, and the National Advisor of Youth. He has been imprisoned and threatened various times.

His story reached believers around the world who prayed for him, his family, and his church. On March 2, 1996, he was released early and placed under house arrest.

Upon his release, Pastor Vila shared about his time in prison:

"I am so thankful for the power of prayer. I received strength from God and was never ill — no flu, no skin disease, no illness at all. And I had lots of opportunities to share the Gospel with my fellow inmates."

Through your faithful prayers and the generous response of the Spirit of Jesus Christ, everything he wants to do in and through me will be done. I can hardly wait to continue on my course.

Paul the Apostle
Martyred in Rome, AD 65
(PHILIPPIANS 1:19,20 THE MESSAGE)

Making Every Minute Count

Patrick Hamilton
23 years old
Scotland
1527

The handsome young man on the scaffold turned to his servant and comforted him, saying, "What I am about to suffer, dear friend, appears fearful and bitter to the flesh. But remember, it is the entrance to everlasting life, which none shall possess who deny their Lord."

Young Patrick Hamilton had all he needed for success: born of royal blood, he was intelligent and talented, pleasant and gentle. While at school, he embraced the teachings of Martin Luther. With Luther he felt that the Bible, not edicts of the established church, held the true foundation for the Christian faith and the relationship of each person to God. Soon his views got him in trouble with the local church government and the crown, so he escaped to Germany.

There, at the University of Marburg, he experienced a great change. Where before he had been sceptical and timid, he now became courageous. Each day he increased in knowledge and, inflamed with godliness, decided to return to Scotland to take the truth of God's Word to his own countrymen.

When he returned to Scotland, he immediately began to preach the truths he had learned. After a short time, he was ordered to appear before the Archbishop. He was so on fire with his message that he did not want to wait for his appointment, but came very early in the morning.

Although he argued powerfully, he was arrested and put in prison. Many tried to get Hamilton to change his mind, or at least to convince him to stop preaching his beliefs and disturbing the established church. But he did not back down from his stand. In fact, his faith was so contagious that a priest who visited his cell was also converted.

The day came for him to be sentenced to death. That same day, after dinner, he was led away to be burned at the stake.

When his executioners had difficulty keeping the fire lit, he used it as one last opportunity to preach to those who were standing near. "How long, O God," he cried, "shall darkness cover this kingdom? How long will You allow this tyranny of men?"

At last, the fire consumed him. As he died, he cried out, "Lord Jesus, receive my spirit."

The day Hamilton was burned at the stake, someone dared to say to his persecutors:

"If you are going to burn any more, you had better do it in a cellar, for the smoke of Hamilton's burning has opened the eyes of hundreds."

Jesus Freaks make the most of every opportunity to share Jesus. Patrick Hamilton preached in prison and at the stake. Do you make your opportunities count for eternity?

Act like people with good sense and not like fools.
These are evil times, so make every minute count...find
out what the Lord wants you to do.

Paul the Apostle
Martyred in Rome, AD 65
(EPHESIANS 5:15-17 CEV)

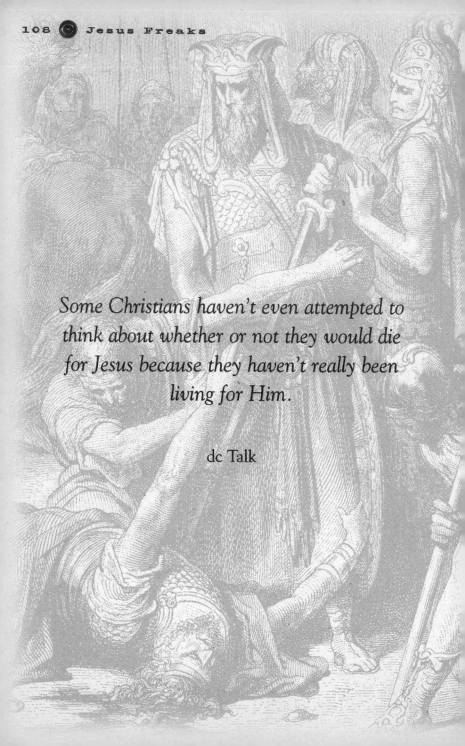

Some Christians haven't even attempted to think about whether or not they would die for Jesus because they haven't really been living for Him.

dc Talk

"We Die With Gratitude"

Chiu-Chin-Hsiu and Ho-Hsiu-Tzu
Jiangxi, Mainland China
During the Red Guard Era, 1966-69

The two Christian girls waited in the Chinese prison yard for the announced execution. A fellow prisoner who watched the scene from his prison cell described their faces as pale but beautiful beyond belief; infinitely sad but sweet. Humanly speaking, they were fearful. But Chiu-Chin-Hsiu and Ho-Hsiu-Tzu had decided to submit to death without renouncing their faith.

Flanked by renegade guards, the executioner came with a revolver in his hand. It was their own pastor! He had been sentenced to die with the two girls. But, as on many other occasions in Church history, the persecutors worked on him, tempting him. They promised to release him if he would shoot the girls. He accepted.

The girls whispered to each other, then bowed respectfully before their pastor. One of them said, "Before you shoot us, we wish to thank you heartily for what you have meant to us. You baptized us, you taught us the ways of eternal life, you gave us holy communion with the same hand in which you now hold the gun.

"You also taught us that Christians are sometimes weak and commit terrible sins, but they can be forgiven again. When you regret what you are about to do to us, do not despair like Judas, but repent like Peter. God bless you, and remember that our last thought was not one of indignation against your failure. Everyone passes through hours of darkness.

"May God reward you for all the good you have done to us. We die with gratitude."

They bowed again.

The pastor's heart was hardened. He shot the girls.

Afterwards he was shot by the Communists.

What does a Jesus Freak do when betrayed by someone close to them? They show them God's love.

Love [God's love in us]...takes no account of the evil done to it — pays no attention to a suffered wrong...Love bears up under anything and everything that comes, is ever ready to believe the best of every person, its hopes are fadeless under all circumstances and it endures everything [without weakening].

Paul the Apostle
Martyred in Rome, AD 65
(1 CORINTHIANS 13:5,7 AMP)

"God Will Give Me Strength"

Rowland Taylor
England
1555

"Rowland, don't go," his friends urged. "You have done your duty. You have testified to the truth and resisted the priest when he tried to bring again his idolatry. Our Saviour Christ told us that when they persecute us in one city, we should flee into another. Keep yourself for another time, when the Church shall have great need of such diligent teachers and godly pastors."

Dr. Taylor replied, "God will not forsake His Church. He will raise up others to teach His people.

"As for me, I believe, before God, I shall never be able to do God so good service, as I may do now; nor shall I ever have so glorious a calling as I now have, nor so great mercy of God offered to me, as now. So I ask you, and all other of my friends, to pray for me; and I know God will give me strength and His Holy Spirit."

By the mid 1500s, the Bible had been translated into English. The town of Hadley was one of the first places to receive the Word of God in all of England. Here, many had often read the whole Bible through and followed God's Word in their living.

But when King Edward died, freedom of religion took a giant step backward. Dr. Rowland Taylor, pastor of Hadley, bravely challenged those who tried to force believers back into the Dark Ages of superstition and idolatry. For this, he was ordered to appear before the bishop and Lord Chancellor.

"I am old and have already lived too long to see these terrible and most wicked days," he told his friends. "You do as your conscience leads you. I am fully determined with God's grace to go to the bishop. I am not expecting justice or truth, but imprisonment and cruel death. Yet I know my cause to be good and righteous and the truth is strong upon my side."

With these words, he willingly went to London where, as predicted, he was accused as a heretic and thrown into prison. After two years, he was again brought before the bishops and given a chance to change his stand.

He answered boldly, "I will not depart from the truth which they had preached in King Edward's days. I thank God for calling me to be worthy to suffer for His Word and truth."

When the bishops saw him so boldly, constantly, and immovably fixed in the truth, they sentenced him to death.

He was immediately sent back to his home town of Hadley to be burned at the stake. Along the way he was so joyful and merry that anyone watching would have thought he was going to a banquet or a wedding. His words to his guards often caused them to weep as he earnestly called them to repent from their evil and wicked living. They marvelled to see him so steadfast, fearless, joyful, and glad to die.

Two miles out of town, he got off his horse and did a little dance, he was so glad to be close to home. He then prayed, "Thank You, Lord, that once more I will see my flock, whom I have most heartily loved and truly taught. Bless them and keep them steadfast in Your Word and truth."

He had to pass through the town to get to the place of execution. On either side of the street were women and men, weeping and crying. "Ah, Lord! There goes our good shepherd, who so faithfully taught us, cared for us, and governed us. O merciful God! What shall we poor, scattered lambs do? What shall come of this most wicked world? Lord, strengthen him and comfort him."

When they reached the place where he would be burned, Dr. Taylor said to all gathered there, "I have taught you nothing but God's holy Word and those lessons that I have taken out of God's blessed book, the holy Bible. I am come here this day to seal it with my blood."

As he kneeled down and prayed, a poor woman stepped in and prayed with him; but they pushed her away and threatened to trample her with the horses. Even so, she would not leave, but stayed and prayed with him.

He went to the stake, kissed it, and stood against it, with his hands folded together and his eyes towards heaven. And so he continually prayed.

They bound him with chains, and several men put the sticks in place, one cruelly throwing a bundle of sticks at Dr. Taylor, so that it hit him on the head, and made blood run down his face. He said, "O friend, I have harm enough; why did you need to do that?"

At last they lit the fire. Dr. Taylor held up both his hands and called upon God, saying, "Merciful Father of heaven, for Jesus Christ my Saviour's sake, receive my soul into Thy hands."

He stood in the flames without either crying or moving, his hands folded together. To spare him further suffering, a man from the town ran towards the fire and struck him on the head with a long-handled battle axe. Taylor died instantly, his corpse falling into the fire.

A Jesus Freak never faces his problems alone. God's Holy Spirit is always there to give him comfort, strength, and hope.

Look at my servant, whom I strengthen. He is my chosen one, and I am pleased with him. I have put my Spirit upon him.

Isaiah 42:1 NLT

Making a Better World

Lieutenant Grecu
Romania
circa 1948

The tough young lieutenant faced Richard Wurmbrand, questioning him on his many activities with the underground church. After accusing him of lying about his contacts, Grecu ordered him to write out all the rules Wurmbrand had broken while in prison.

Wurmbrand willingly sat at the table writing out his "Declaration." It had been two years since he had held a pen, so it was difficult to write. After he had listed all the rules he had broken, he ended his confession with, "I have never spoken against the Communists. I am a disciple of Christ, who has given us love for our enemies. I understand them and pray for their conversion so that they will become my brothers in the faith."

Lieutenant Grecu had been indoctrinated with the belief that Communism was the answer to the world's problems. He sincerely believed that he was making a better world, but when he read the "Declaration," he was overwhelmed. How could Wurmbrand write of his love for a government that had put him in prison and tortured him for so many years?

Grecu scoffed, "This is one of your Christian commandments that no one can keep."

Wurmbrand looked at the Lieutenant, his eyes filled with the love of God, and responded, "It's not a matter of keeping a commandment. When I became a Christian, it was as if I had been reborn, with a new character full of love. Just as only water can flow from a spring, so only love can come from a loving heart."

Over the years, Wurmbrand had many other opportunities to talk about God's love with Lieutenant Grecu. Before he was released, in his own prison cell, Wurmbrand had the wonderful privilege of seeing Grecu confess Christ.

Jesus Freaks love their enemies. Others say it is too hard — impossible in fact — which is true, unless God does it for you and through you. It is not ever easy to pray for your enemies, but it works.

As you pray for prisoners in restricted countries around the world, pray that God's love will be evident in their lives and that it would change the hearts of their tormentors as it changed Lieutenant Grecu.

God, accept all my sufferings, my
tiredness, my humiliations, my tears, my
nostalgia, my being hungry, my suffering
of cold, all the bitterness accumulated in
my soul....

Dear Lord, have pity on those who
persecute and torture us day and night.
Grant them, too, the divine grace of
knowing the sweetness and happiness of
Your love.

Woman prisoner in Siberia
Vorkuta, U.S.S.R.
circa 1960s

Die With Us!

Haim and his family
Cambodia
circa 1970s

All during the night, the members of Haim's family comforted each other. They knew they only had a few more hours to live on this earth. The Cambodian Communist soldiers had tied them all together and forced them to lie down on the grass.

Earlier that day, Haim's whole family had been rounded up for execution. Because they were all Christians, the Communists considered them "bad blood" and "enemies of the glorious revolution."

In the morning, they were made to dig their own graves.

The killers were generous. They allowed their victims a moment of prayer to prepare themselves for death. Parents and children held hands and knelt together near the open grave.

After his family finished their prayers, Haim exhorted the Communists and all those looking on to repent and to receive Jesus as Saviour.

Suddenly, one of Haim's young sons leapt to his feet, bolted to the nearby forest, and disappeared.

Haim was amazingly cool as he persuaded the soldiers not to chase the boy but to allow him to call the boy back. While the family knelt, the father pleaded with his son to return and die with them.

"Think my son," he shouted. "Can stealing a few more days of life, as a fugitive in that forest, compare to joining your family here around a grave, but soon free forever in paradise?"

Weeping, the boy walked back.

Haim said to the executioners, "Now we are ready to go." But none of the soldiers would kill them.

Finally, an officer who had not witnessed the scene came and shot the Christians.

Atheists — those who don't believe in God or life after death — are amazed when Christians are ready to sacrifice their lives rather than deny a God no one can see. They don't understand the deep work of the Holy Spirit and how He makes both the Father's love and heaven an undeniable reality in the heart of a believer.

For his Holy Spirit speaks to us deep in our hearts and tells us that we are God's children. And since we are his children, we will share his treasures — for everything God gives to his Son, Christ, is ours, too. But if we are to share his glory, we must also share his suffering. Yet what we suffer now is nothing compared to the glory he will give us later.

Paul the Apostle
Beheaded in Rome, AD 65
(ROMANS 8:16-18 NLT)

"This Is the Truth"

Group of children
Sudan
1993

An American TV journalist interviewed a group of children from a Sunday school in southern Sudan where Arab Muslims regularly raided their village and slaughtered Christians. Many of their relatives had already been killed.

The journalist asked, "Would you turn to Islam? Or would you prefer to die for Christ? If so, why?"

They replied, "We will remain Christians because this is the truth." As they spoke, their faces seemed to glow with light just like Stephen, Christianity's first martyr, whose face "was like that of an angel."

I know the Lord is always with me.

I will not be shaken, for he is right beside me.

No wonder my heart is filled with joy,

and my mouth shouts his praises!

You will show me the way of life,

granting me the joy of your presence

and the pleasures of living with you forever.

Psalm 16:8,9,11 NLT

Unwilling to Pay
the Price

Natasha Lazareva
U.S.S.R.
circa 1970s

The Communists held two photos before Natasha's eyes. One showed Aida Skripnikova, in the movie-star beauty of her youth. The second showed the terrible effects of Soviet prison life. Aida Skripnikova's youthful loveliness was gone. She smiled with cracked lips and a pale face. She looked like an old woman. The contrast between the two photos was so overwhelming that Natasha had to look away.

Natasha, the creator of a Russian Christian underground magazine, had already been sent to jail once. When she was released, she began printing the magazine again, secretly, and again she was arrested. This time she could be given a heavy sentence.

The Communists then showed her the picture of Sadunaite, a young Catholic nun, followed by one of her drab face when she was freed. They showed her a picture of Viltchinskaya, who by the age of 21 had lost all her teeth and hair because of the poor food and lack of sunlight while confined to her prison cell and working in the slave labour camps.

"This is what awaits you," they told Natasha, "unless you cooperate with us and denounce all your co-workers."

To save her own physical beauty, Natasha gave the Communists the names of fifty other Christians. She put her co-workers in the underground church at risk for prison and torture. She was still sentenced to six years in prison.

Natasha forgot about Mary Magdalene, tears smearing her makeup, anointing Jesus' feet with her costliest perfume and using her own hair as a cloth to rub it in. She forgot about Mary, Jesus' mother, brokenhearted, weeping bitterly at the foot of the cross, concerned more about her suffering Son than her hair or personal appearance.

She also forgot about Jesus, the fairest, with His face swollen from beatings and soiled with spittle, His body trembling with fatigue and bleeding all over, who sacrificed His own appearance to the point that He had "no beauty that we should desire Him" (Isaiah 53:2 NKJV).

What would you have done?

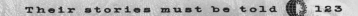

He is no fool who gives what he cannot keep to gain what he cannot lose.

Jim Elliot
Speared by headhunters in Ecuador
while serving there as a missionary
1956

"More Love to Thee"

Pastor Kim and his congregation
North Korea
1950s

For years, Pastor Kim and 27 of his flock of Korean saints had lived in hand-dug tunnels beneath the earth. Then, as the Communists were building a road, they discovered the Christians living underground.

The officials brought them out before a crowd of 30,000 in the village of Gok San for a public trial and execution. They were told, "Deny Christ, or you will die." But they refused.

At this point the head Communist officer ordered four children from the group seized and had them prepared for hanging. With ropes tied around their small necks, the officer again commanded the parents to deny Christ.

Not one of the believers would deny their faith. They told the children, "We will soon see you in heaven." The children died quietly.

The officer then called for a steamroller to be brought in. He forced the Christians to lie on the ground in its path. As its engine revved, they were given one last chance to recant their faith in Jesus. Again they refused.

As the steamroller began to inch forward, the Christians began to sing a song they had often sung together. As their bones and bodies were crushed under the pressure of the massive rollers, their lips uttered the words:

"More love to Thee, O Christ, more love to Thee
Thee alone I seek, more love to Thee

Let sorrow do its work, more love to Thee
Then shall my latest breath whisper Thy praise
This be the parting cry my heart shall raise;
More love, O Christ, to Thee."

The execution was reported in the North Korean press as an act of suppressing superstition.

Throughout history, Jesus Freaks have sung during their final moments on earth. To the astonishment of their tormentors, they joyfully raised their voices in praise to God.

For our present troubles are quite small and won't last very long. Yet they produce for us an immeasurably great glory that will last forever! So we don't look at the troubles we can see right now; rather, we look forward to what we have not yet seen. For the troubles we see will soon be over, but the joys to come will last forever.

Paul the Apostle
Written after having been
imprisoned, stoned and left for
dead, shipwrecked, and tortured
numerous times by those who
opposed him
(2 CORINTHIANS 4:17,18 NLT)

Without fear we sang in prisons 30 feet beneath the earth. We were terribly hungry, beaten, and tortured.

The Communists were good at torturing us.

We would say to each other, "The Communists beat us very well — let us do our work well. Let us sing well."

Richard Wurmbrand
Spent 14 years in a Communist prison
Romania, 1940s, 50s, and 60s

Missionary to Terrorists

Francisco
22 years old
Peru
1990

"I want to bring Senderista terrorists to Christ!" The young Bible student's eyes burned with his desire. His city, Lima, Peru, had swelled to seven million as people fled from the countryside because the Senderistas were murdering so many.

"I do not want to flee. I want to attack with the Gospel!" he exclaimed.

God answered the prayers of this Jesus Freak.

One day, as Francisco was walking past the national palace, a car sped by. A mortar launched a bomb from the car which exploded in the palace. Then the car vanished.

Immediately, Peruvian police swarmed throughout the area. Francisco was arrested and taken to the maximum security prison. He was locked up on the fourth floor, in an area set aside exclusively for holding the Senderistas. Five hundred men and women — all terrorists — were imprisoned in this area.

Francisco wasted no time grieving over his circumstances. He was prepared. He had diligently studied how to present the Gospel to Communist revolutionaries. In a gentle way, he began preaching to the terrorists, sharing the love of God.

A pretty woman named Maria listened carefully. She was a 24-year-old student from San Marcos University in Lima. One of Maria's tasks with the Senderistas had been to take her pistol and shoot the wounded victims through their skull to guarantee their death.

"Could God possibly love and forgive me?" she wondered. When Maria prayed a sinner's prayer with Francisco, she found out He definitely could — and that He did!

A year passed while Francisco waited for his trial. During that time, he brought over sixty terrorists to Jesus! As the love of God penetrated hardened hearts, terrorists became children of God.

There is now a church in this prison, filled with new believers brought to Jesus Christ through the faithfulness of Francisco.

Francisco's prayer was answered in an unusual way — but what safer place could there be to minister to terrorists than in jail? Francisco was quick to recognize that God had changed evil to good: He used Francisco's wrongful imprisonment to give him the desire of his heart. Then God blessed his efforts, and many were brought into the kingdom of God.

You intended to harm me, but God intended it for good to accomplish what is now being done, the saving of many lives.

Joseph
Sold into slavery and later
imprisoned
circa 1689 BC
(GENESIS 50:20 NIV)

Everything happening to me in this jail only serves to make Christ more accurately known, regardless of whether I live or die. They didn't shut me up; they gave me a pulpit! Alive, I'm Christ's messenger; dead, I'm his bounty. Life versus even more life! I can't lose.

Paul the Apostle
Martyred in Rome, AD 65
(PHILIPPIANS 1:20,21 THE MESSAGE)

Lifted From the Fire

Fritz Manampiring
Indonesia
1997

The small mob surrounded the church. Holding rocks in each hand, they clapped the stones together furiously. The radical Muslims were like mad men carrying out a holy pilgrimage of terror.

A policeman begged Pastor Fritz Manampiring, "Pastor, please don't hold a service here today. This is what the Muslim leaders want. They have become crazy!"

Not desiring to stir up any more trouble, Pastor Fritz assured the police officer that they would not have services. As members of the congregation arrived, Fritz shouted to them to go back to their homes. But before the church members could respond, the mob erupted, their stones flying. As the Muslims attacked the church, they chanted, "Allah-u-Akbar!" (Allah is mighty!)

Like Saul before his conversion, these men believed they were serving God. They were punishing infidels, those who blasphemed. The police tried to stop the mob, but with little success. These Muslims were fixed on persecuting the followers of Jesus.

The mob dragged Fritz's wife outside, beating and kicking her. If the security officers hadn't stopped them, Pastor Fritz and his wife would have been killed.

The officers took Fritz and his wife to the military office for their safety. Fritz filed a report, but no arrests were made. No one would have blamed Fritz or his wife if they had left town or stopped their church services altogether. But they had pastored there for over ten years. They loved their congregation, so despite the threat of future persecution, they remained in the area to minister the Gospel.

Two weeks later, a security officer warned Pastor Fritz of another attack by radical Muslims. That evening the mob arrived, bigger and angrier than before. This time, they were ready for *jihad* or holy war. Again they surrounded the church, which was also Pastor Fritz's home, and began to throw stones, yelling, "Attack! Attack!"

This time, the police did not show up to protect Fritz's family. It didn't take the mob long to enter the church and ransack everything in sight. They cut off the electricity, leaving the rooms in darkness. Before Fritz and his wife could escape, someone hit his wife across the back of the head with a club. Fritz was clubbed until his face was drenched in blood.

The Muslims then tied Fritz with steel wire and continued to beat him. Fritz cried out, "Lord Jesus, help!" One of the attackers forced his burning cigarette into Fritz's mouth. Laughing and jeering, he told Fritz, "Eat your Jesus!"

A hood was placed over the pastor's head, and he was taken outside and stripped naked. Attackers beat him, burned him with cigarettes, and rolled him through the broken glass from the church window. Others continued to destroy his home and church. The chants of the attackers echoed in his ears, "*Allah-u-Akbar! Allah-u-Akbar!*" Finally, a blow to his jaw was more than he could bear, and Fritz fell unconscious.

When he awoke, he found himself lying on a pile of wood from the ruined church. His attackers were throwing shattered furniture on top of him. He was soon choking from smoke as flames emerged around him. Fritz prayed what he thought was his final prayer before meeting his Lord face-to-face, "Lord, I give my soul and spirit to you."

Fritz doesn't remember how it happened, but he suddenly found himself being lifted from the blaze. Like Shadrach, Meshach, and Abednego, God had spared him from the flames. After Fritz escaped the fire, he was tied to a pole, stoned, and left for dead. He suffered a concussion, his jaw was smashed, and nerves in his eyes were permanently damaged, but Fritz refused to give up and die.

Fritz and his wife are now staying with friends near where their church and home were destroyed. Not surprisingly, he continues to pastor the flock.

They defeated him (Satan) through the blood of the Lamb and the bold word of their witness. They weren't in love with themselves; they were willing to die for Christ.

John the Apostle
Tortured & exiled, AD 97
Roman Empire
(REVELATION 12:11 THE MESSAGE)

"A Christian Is Chosen by Jesus Christ"

Mehdi Dibaj
Iran
1994

"Men choose a religion, but a Christian is chosen by Jesus Christ. To be a Christian means to belong to Christ. Jesus asked me to renounce even my life, to follow Him faithfully, not to fear the world even if my body must perish. I prefer to know that God, the Almighty, is with me, even if it means that the whole world is against me.

"I am in God's hands. For 45 years I have walked with the God of miracles, and His goodness is for me a shadow that protects me in His love.

"The God of Daniel, who protected his friends, protected me during my nine years in prison, and all torments changed to my good, so that I have the fullness of love and gratitude.

"Of all the prophets, Jesus alone was resurrected from the dead, and He remains our living Mediator forever. I gave my life into His hands. For me, life is an opportunity to serve Him, and death is the privilege of getting to be with Him."

Pastor Mehdi Dibaj of Iran was on trial for his life, and these words were the defence he gave in court. An upper-class Muslim, he and his family had converted to Christianity. He had dared to translate Christian radio programmes and books into the Farsi language. He was arrested in 1985 and accused of apostasy, denying the Muslim faith. For this, he faced the death penalty.

In Iran, social and political pressure is sometimes used to force Christians to recant their new-found faith in Jesus Christ. Some are even tortured. Dibaj was imprisoned alone for two years in a cramped hole with no room to stretch his legs. While he was in prison, his wife, Azizeh, left Dibaj and was forced to marry a Muslim.

When Dibaj steadfastly refused to deny his faith, the court condemned him to death. But after one month he was set free because of international attention that had been brought to his case. Soon after this, however, he was found dead in a park. It is believed by some that Islamic leaders had called for his execution.

Despite losing their father, his four children remain faithful to Jesus Christ.

As he faced the court that would sentence him to death, Pastor Dibaj said, "I prefer to know that God, the Almighty, is with me, even if it means that the whole world is against me." He had learned the secret of being able to stand alone among men — standing with God.

Pray for radio programmes that preach the Gospel to Muslims. Pray for safety for all those involved. Pray for the listeners, that the Word of God will penetrate their darkness and bring them to new life in Jesus Christ.

Death is much sweeter to me with the testimony of truth than life with the least denial.

Geleazium
Martyred in St. Angelo, Italy
Middle Ages

Like Gold in the Fire

Polycarp
Smyrna (now Izmar, Turkey)
AD 168

The kindly, old bishop entered the arena under armed guard. The stands were filled with an angry mob; their shouts filled the air.

Suddenly, a voice from heaven spoke to the bishop, saying, "Be strong, Polycarp, and play the man." Despite the noise from the crowd, many of those who stood nearby also heard the heavenly voice.

Once inside the arena, the soldiers quickly brought Polycarp before the Roman proconsul. Polycarp, the well-known Bishop of Smyrna, was the last living link with the twelve apostles, as he had studied under John. As soon as the crowd learned that this famous bishop had been arrested, a great cheer went up.

The proconsul tried to get Polycarp to deny Jesus Christ: "Swear by the fortune of Caesar. Take the oath and I will release you. Curse Christ!"

The bishop stood firm. "Eighty-six years have I served the Lord Jesus Christ, and He never once wronged me. How can I blaspheme my King who has saved me?"

The proconsul threatened, "I have wild beasts ready, and I will throw you to them if you do not change your mind."

"Let them come, for my purpose is unchangeable," replied Polycarp.

"If the wild beasts don't scare you, then I will burn you with fire," said the proconsul.

"You threaten me with a fire which will burn for an hour and then will go out, but you are ignorant of the fire of the future judgment of God reserved for the everlasting torment of the ungodly. But why do you delay? Bring on the beasts, or the fire, or whatever you choose; you shall not move me to deny Christ, my Lord and Saviour."

When the proconsul saw that Polycarp would not recant, he sent the herald to proclaim three times in the middle of the stadium, "Polycarp has professed himself a Christian."

As soon as they heard these words, the whole multitude of Gentiles and Jews furiously demanded that he be burned alive. Immediately dry wood was brought out and heaped in the centre of the arena for a bonfire.

When they were about to nail him to the stake, Polycarp said, "Leave me as I am; He who gives me strength to endure the fire will enable me to remain still within the fire." They agreed to this and simply tied his hands behind his back with a rope.

In his final prayer, he prayed, "O Father, I thank You, that You have called me to this day and hour and have counted me worthy to receive my place among the number of the holy martyrs. Amen."

As soon as he uttered the word, "Amen," the officers lit the fire. The flames rose high above his body, but miraculously, he was not burned. Those who watched said, "He was in the midst of the fire, not as burning flesh but as gold and silver refined in a furnace. And we smelled such a sweet aroma as of incense or some other precious spice."

Since the fire did not hurt him, the executioner was ordered to stab him with a sword. As soon as he did, so much blood flowed from the wound that it put out the fire.

In the book of Revelation, John was instructed by the Lord to write on a scroll and send it to the seven churches. Here's what John wrote to the church at Smyrna:

Do not fear any of those things which you are about to suffer. Indeed, the devil is about to throw some of you into prison, that you may be tested, and you will have tribulation ten days. Be faithful until death, and I will give you the crown of life.

John the Apostle
Tortured and exiled, AD 97
Roman Empire
(REVELATION 2:10 NKJV)

Crazy for Jesus

Yun
16 years old
Mainland China
1950s

"There is a book that tells how to get to heaven?"

"Yes, Yun. I have seen it with my own eyes," answered the old man.

"Where is this book?" asked Yun. "I must see it for myself!"

"It is far away — over 35 miles," the old man said sadly. "It is too far to walk, and you have no bicycle."

"I will go!" replied Yun. This young man walked the 35 miles and met with the owner of the Bible. Eventually he was able to get a Bible of his own.

Yun then joined with another Christian, and together they went from village to village telling about Jesus. As this was illegal, the police would often come to stop them.

Yun came up with a way around this problem. He had read in 1 Samuel 21:13 that David once pretended to be crazy to escape from his enemies. When the police came, Yun did the same thing: he made a spectacle of himself. The police laughed at him and let him go. After they were gone, he would become serious again and continue to speak to the people about salvation.

Before long, however, Yun was cruelly beaten and put in prison for his faith. Afterwards, he had to stand public trial in a marketplace.

Yun was small and thin. He was dressed in rags and barefoot, his face deformed from the beatings. The judge said to him, "We will give you one last chance to save your life. If you leave the underground church and join the Three-Self Patriotic Church, we will make you one of its leaders."

Yun remained silent. He knew the government church worked closely with the Communists and often turned house-church Christians in to be imprisoned or beaten.

The judge brought in a doctor who said to him sarcastically, "I will heal your dumbness!" The doctor forced needles under Yun's fingernails.

When Yun passed out, the policemen walked on his body saying, "Your stubbornness led to this."

He was brought back to a cell where other prisoners urinated on him. His only treasure was a tin cup on which he had painted a cross. This was thrown in the toilet. Weeping, he fished it out and pressed it to his heart.

Yun fasted often, praying for the Chinese churches, his fellow inmates, and himself. He was finally released after ten years, still strong in faith and refusing any compromise with the world or with the government-supported church.

God deliberately chose things the world considers foolish in order to shame those who think they are wise...so that no one can ever boast in the presence of God...As the Scriptures say, "The person who wishes to boast should boast only of what the Lord has done."

Paul the Apostle
Beheaded in Rome, AD 65
(1 CORINTHIANS 1:27,29,31 NLT)

"I Rest in the Arms of God"

Nadejda Sloboda
U.S.S.R.
circa 1960s

"You must come to my house tonight and listen to the radio with us," Nadejda whispered to her neighbour. "I have never heard anything like it before. A man is preaching God's Word from the Bible. I don't know how it happened, but these broadcasts have changed my life!"

Nadejda Sloboda was the first one in her village to be converted through Gospel broadcasting in Russia from stations in neighbouring countries. Soon, her love for God and her zealous witness brought others to Christ. Although she wasn't a pastor, she formed a church in her village.

As time passed, this church grew so mightily that the police had to surround the village to keep people of the nearby collective farms from coming to hear the Gospel message.

For this, Sister Sloboda was sentenced to four years of prison. Her five children were forcibly taken away to an atheistic boarding school. Her husband was left alone.

In prison, Sister Sloboda told other prisoners about Christ. For this, she was confined in an unheated, isolated cell, where she had to sleep on the cold, concrete floor without a mattress. Prisoners find it impossible to sleep in such conditions: Even the walls are too cold to lean against comfortably. Some report that by standing with just their forehead touching the wall, they could manage to sleep enough to survive for a few days.

Yet Sister Sloboda was kept in this cell for two months! Not only that, during the day she was put to hard labour with the other prisoners. The Communists expected that the lack of sleep combined with the hard labour would completely ruin her health and break her resolve to stand for her faith. Yet she never weakened.

Everybody asked, "How can you endure it?"

She answered, "I fall asleep on the cold concrete floor trusting in God and it becomes warm around me.

"I rest in the arms of God."

The eternal God is your refuge, and underneath are the everlasting arms.

Deuteronomy 33:27 NIV

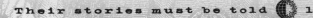

Humanly speaking, we know that no one likes to suffer physically. But I know that if the Lord leads me into it, He will give me the strength to survive it.

Pastor Li De Xian
Mainland China
1990s

"I Have to Know"

Thomas Hauker
England
1555

"Thomas," his friend lowered his voice so as not to be heard by the guard. "I have to ask you this favour. I need to know if what the others say about the grace of God is true. Tomorrow, when they burn you at the stake, if the pain is tolerable and your mind is still at peace, lift your hands above your head. Do it right before you die. Thomas, I *have* to know."

Thomas Hauker whispered to his friend, "I will."

The next morning, Hauker was bound to the stake and the fire was lit. The fire burned a long time, but Hauker remained motionless. His skin was burnt to a crisp and his fingers were gone. Everyone watching supposed he was dead. Suddenly, miraculously, Hauker lifted his hands, still on fire, over his head. He reached them up to the living God, and then, with great rejoicing, clapped them together three times.

The people there broke into shouts of praise and applause. Hauker's friend had his answer.

My grace is enough; it's all you need. My strength comes into its own in your weakness.... It was a case of

Christ's strength moving in on my weakness. Now...I just let Christ take over! And so the weaker I get, the stronger I become.

Paul the Apostle
Martyred in Rome, AD 65
(2 CORINTHIANS 12:9,10
THE MESSAGE)

Do your worst, I am a Christian. Christ is
my help and supporter, and thus armed I
will never serve your gods nor do I fear
your authority or that of your master, the
Emperor. Commence your torments as
soon as you please, and make use of every
means that your malignity can invent, and
you shall find in the end that I am not to
be shaken from my resolution.

Andronicus
Roman Empire
AD 303

Andronicus had been thrown into prison because he
was unwilling to deny the Christian faith. Then he was
whipped and his bleeding wounds were rubbed with salt.
He was brought out from prison and tortured again,
thrown to the wild beasts, and finally killed with a sword.
This brave martyr was steadfast to the end.

Making a Lasting Difference

Stenley
Indonesia
1996

Stenley was eager to take on the challenge of the mission field. A recent graduate of Palembang Bible School in Jakarta, the Lord sent him to the very remote island of Mentawai, Indonesia. Here, inhabitants mix witchcraft and the occult with Islam. Stenley was very bold in preaching the Gospel, telling Muslims to burn their idols when they received Jesus Christ.

One day a newly-saved Muslim burned his idol, which contained a rolled-up scroll from the Koran. When area Muslims heard of this, they became very angry and reported Stenley to the officials. He was arrested and thrown in jail.

The pastor of the Bible school heard about Stenley's arrest and went immediately to see him. When Pastor Siwi arrived at the jail, he was told Stenley had been transferred to prison. Days later, when Pastor Siwi finally found Stenley, he found him severely beaten, bruised, and unconscious. Repeated blows to the head had left him in a coma.

Pastor Siwi did what he could to care for Stenley and make him more comfortable. Stenley seemed to revive slightly as he did this. Pastor Siwi asked with tears, "Stenley, this is Pastor Siwi. Can you hear me?" But Stenley could not move or speak. All he could do was lie on his back and cry. Soon after his pastor's visit, Stenley went to be with the Lord.

Stenley's death made a great impact on those who knew him. In the middle of the night, seven of his fellow students went to the Bible school superintendent, requesting that they be sent to preach the Gospel on Mentawai Island, where Stenley died.

His death also impacted his hometown. There, 53 people made decisions to attend Bible school, including Stenley's mother and sister. Soon after they graduate, seven of them are going to evangelize where Stenley died.

His mother was asked, "Are you not afraid to die?"

She answered, "Why should I be afraid to die?"

Stenley's life made a lasting difference on the island of Mentawai. Eleven Muslims there have converted to Christ because of Stenley's faith. There has also been a revival among the more than 300 traditional Christians on the island. Most of them were once bound by alcohol, cigarettes, and gambling, but now their spirits are on fire to seek God and study the Bible.

Pray for the many Christians whose courageous lives and vibrant, fearless witness are making a tremendous impact on nations such as Indonesia. Although they have been burned, harassed, beaten, and imprisoned, they have refused to deny Jesus. Pray for a harvest of souls from the seeds they have sown.

Not Afraid of the Cross

Andrew, Peter's brother
Greece
AD 66

Andrew boldly looked the governor in the eye. "It is good for you, the judge of men, to first know your Judge who dwells in heaven," he said, his voice ringing with the force of truth. "After you know Him, then worship Him, removing from your mind false gods and blind idols."

Christians all over the empire were being executed in obedience to a decree from the Roman Senate. Peter had been crucified a year earlier, and before this year would end, six more of the original disciples, including Andrew, would be executed. Of the twelve, only John would remain on earth.

Andrew had voluntarily come to face Aegaeas, the governor, to persuade him not to persecute the many Christians Andrew had brought to the faith in the city of Patras.

Andrew's words angered the king. "Are you the same Andrew who has overthrown the temple of the gods and persuades men to be of that superstitious sect which Rome has now commanded to be abolished?"

Andrew answered, "The princes of the Romans do not understand the truth. The Son of God, coming from heaven into the world for man's sake, has taught and declared how those idols, whom you so honour as gods, are not gods, but rather cruel devils, enemies to mankind. They teach the people to do things that are so offensive to God that He turns away. In serving the devil, people fall into all kinds of wickedness, and after they die, nothing remains for them but their evil deeds."

"Enough!" the governor commanded. "Do not teach such things anymore or you will be fastened to the cross with all speed."

Andrew answered, "If I were afraid of the death of the cross, I would not have preached about the majesty, honour, and glory of the cross."

The governor then pronounced sentence, "This man is starting a new sect and taking away the religion of the Roman gods. I hereby sentence him to death by crucifixion."

As Andrew was brought towards the place of execution, he saw, from afar off, the cross prepared for him. Instead of the fear that might be expected, fervent love for Jesus rose up in his heart. He cried out, "O cross, most welcome and long looked for! With a willing mind, I joyfully come to you, being the disciple of Him who hung on you." As he neared the cross he said, "The nearer I come to the cross, the nearer I come to God; and the farther I am from the cross, the farther I remain from God."

For three days, the apostle hung on the cross. As long as he could move his tongue, he instructed all who stood nearby, encouraging them, "Remain steadfast in the word and doctrine which you have received, instructing one another, that you may dwell with God in eternity, and receive the fruit of His promises."

After three days, the Christians asked the governor to take Andrew down from the cross and release him to them. But Andrew, hearing their plans, cried out, "O Lord Jesus Christ! Don't let Your servant, who hangs here on the cross

for Your name's sake, be released to dwell again among men!
Please receive me, O my Lord, my God! You I have known,
You I have loved, to You I cling, You I desire to see, and in
You I am what I am."

Having spoken these words, he committed his spirit into
the hands of his heavenly Father.

*I'm about to die, my life an offering on God's altar.
This is the only race worth running. I've run hard right
to the finish, believed all the way. All that's left now is the
shouting — God's applause! Depend on it, he's an honest
judge. He'll do right not only by me, but by everyone eager
for his coming.*

Paul the Apostle
Martyred in Rome, AD 65
(2 TIMOTHY 4:7,8 THE MESSAGE)

Let us keep our eyes steadily upon the goal . . . For when we hear the shout from the skies, all else will fade into utter nothingness. For the Lord shall descend — from heaven with a shout. Even so, come, Lord Jesus.

Robert Jaffray
Parc-Parc Prison, New Guinea
1945

Dr. Robert Jaffray risked his life to take the Gospel to the primitive Dani tribesmen of Dutch New Guinea. He was tortured and died as a prisoner of the Japanese during World War II.

Hatred Traded for Happiness

Idris Miah
Bangladesh
1995

"My name is Idris Miah. I have a wife named Rahana and four girls, ages seven, five, three, and one. I was a good Muslim man, but I knew a bad Muslim man named Abu Bakkar Sidhikki who would often get drunk. No one in our village liked him, but what Abu eventually did made us *hate* him: he became a Christian. Some Christian men had visited his house and told him about Jesus. Abu then accepted Jesus and became a Christian.

"The village leaders met and decided that what he did was so bad that we would have to kick him out of our village and burn down his house. We formed a group of twenty-five men and went to his house. We were sneaking up to his house to take him by surprise.

"As we got closer we could hear him praying. He was actually praying for our whole village. He was asking Jesus to forgive everyone in the village. He said Jesus should forgive us because we did not know what we were doing. This made us angry because we thought we knew what we were doing. Then all twenty-five of us rushed to his house to apprehend him, but there was an invisible force that would not let any of us enter his house to drag him out. We all became scared and everyone ran back to his own house.

"When I got home I could not sleep. I kept thinking about Abu's prayer. He said we did not know what we were doing. Was it true? Was he right? I tossed and turned but could not get this experience out of my mind. Finally, at 3:00 A.M. I could not wait any longer. I went back to Abu's house and said, 'Who is Jesus?'

"He told me how Jesus gave his life for sinners and how I could be saved. After three hours of this, I asked Jesus to forgive me and I surrendered my life to him. Jesus saved me!

"I rushed to my house and shared what happened to me with my wife and she also became a Christian along with my children.

"As the news of our conversion spread, the village leaders, including my father-in-law, condemned us. They said that no one can hire me to work in their fields. I am poor and do not own any land to farm myself. If no one will hire me, how can I support my family?

"They said they will give me seven days to change my mind and become a Muslim again, or they will kick us out of the village. Thank God they haven't done this yet. My children have already been kicked out of school because we became Christians.

"I have the joy of Jesus in my heart. I give my life and my family to Jesus. I hope this gift is acceptable to my Lord."

If people persecute you because you are a Christian, don't curse them; pray that God will bless them. When others are happy, be happy with them. If they are sad, share their sorrow...

Don't let evil get the best of you, but conquer evil by doing good.

> Paul the Apostle
> Martyred in Rome, AD 65
> (ROMANS 12:14,15,21 NLT)

Angels are transparent. If an angel stands before you with a man behind him, the presence of the angel does not keep you from seeing the man. On the contrary: Looking at a man through an angel makes him more beautiful.

I see my torturers through an angel. In that way, even they become lovable.

Ivan "Vanya" Moiseyev
Martyred in the U.S.S.R., 1972

Smiling at Her Torturer

Liuba Ganevskaya
U.S.S.R.
1970s

"Enough is enough," Liuba Ganevskaya said to herself. "I will not receive the blows with meekness anymore. Tonight, if they begin again, I will tell the guard to his face that he is a criminal."

Liuba, arrested for her faith by the Russian Communists, was kept in a solitary cell, starved, and beaten. Still, she had not denied Jesus or revealed the names of other believers. As so many others, she had patiently suffered for the sake of the Gospel.

She promised herself that tonight would be different.

But that night, when the guard insulted her with foul words and was just about to start beating her, she somehow saw him differently.

She noticed, for the first time, that he was as tired of beating her as she was of being beaten. She was worn out from lack of sleep and so was he. He was as desperate over not getting any information from her as she was about suffering for refusing to betray her friends.

A voice told her, "He is so much like you. You are both caught in the same drama of life. Stalin, the chief Communist dictator, killed thousands of God's children, but he also killed 10,000 officers of his own secret police. Three successive heads of the police — Yagoda, Yezhov, and Beria — were shot by their comrades, just like the Christians they had persecuted!

"You and your torturers pass through the same vale of tears."

Liuba looked up at the guard who had already lifted his whip to beat her. She smiled.

Stunned, he asked, "Why do you smile?"

She replied, "I don't see you the way a mirror would show you right now. I see you as you surely once were, a beautiful, innocent child. We are the same age. We might have been playmates.

"I see you, too, as I hope you will be. There was once a persecutor worse than you named Saul of Tarsus. He became an apostle and a saint."

The torturer put down his whip.

She continued, "What burden so weighs on you that it drives you to the madness of beating a person who has done you no harm?"

He had no answer. The torturer left that day a changed man.

A gentle response defuses anger.

Proverbs 15:1 THE MESSAGE

Such love has no fear because perfect love expels all fear. If we are afraid, it is for fear of judgment, and this shows that his love has not been perfected in us. We love each other as a result of his loving us first.

John the Apostle
Exiled to Patmos, AD 95
(1 JOHN 4:18,19 NLT)

Jesus does not promise that when we bless our enemies
and do good to them they will not despise us and
persecute us. They certainly will.

But not even that can hurt us or overcome us, so long
as we pray for them. For if we pray for them, we are
taking their distress and poverty, guilt and perdition
upon ourselves, and pleading to God for them.

Every insult they utter only serves to bind us more
closely to God and them. Their persecution of us only
serves to bring them nearer to reconciliation with God
and to further the triumphs of love.

It is only when one sees the anger and wrath of God
hanging like grim realities over the head of one's
enemies that one can know something of what it means
to love them and forgive them.

Dietrich Bonhoeffer
Hanged in Nazi Germany
1945

Bonhoeffer courageously took a stand to protect Jews
against persecution in Nazi Germany, saying, "Christ wills
that the weak and persecuted should be rescued, and He
must be obeyed." Because of this stand, he could no longer
support the German state church. He helped create a new
group called the "Confessing Church" and led an "illegal"
seminary. He eventually became active in the resistance
movement, which led to his arrest and execution.

Gospel Flames

Ten Christians
Mainland China
During the Red Guard Era, 1966–69

Ten brothers and sisters in Christ were imprisoned, beaten, and bound. They had preached with tears streaming down, causing the passers-by and street-sellers, Christians and non-Christians, to stand still and listen. Even the fortune-tellers were moved by the Holy Spirit and burst out crying. Many people hearing the Word forgot to eat, work, or even return home.

The brothers and sisters preached until they were exhausted, but the crowd would not let them leave. The authorities, however, came and dragged the Christians away one by one, binding them with ropes and beating them with electric-shock poles, knocking them unconscious. When they revived, they continued to pray, sing, and preach to the bystanders.

When they were bound and beaten, many people noticed a strange expression on their faces, and the crowd saw to their amazement that they were smiling. Their spirit and appearance were so lively and gracious that many were led to believe in Jesus by their example.

When the brothers and sisters in that area saw them bound and forced to kneel on the ground for more than three days without food or water, beaten with sticks until their faces were covered with blood, their hands made black by the ropes — but still praying, singing, and praising the Lord

— then they too wished to share persecution. In this area recently, the flame of the Gospel has spread everywhere!

Because I preach this Good News, I am suffering and have been chained like a criminal. But the word of God cannot be chained.

I am willing to endure anything if it will bring salvation and eternal glory in Christ Jesus to those God has chosen.

Paul the Apostle
Martyred in Rome, AD 65
(2 TIMOTHY 2:9,10 NLT)

Indestructible John

John the Apostle
Roman Empire
AD 95

"This is John, the apostle of Jesus Christ!" the herald proclaimed three times. Hearing this, the crowd in the stadium cheered wildly. They had gathered to see how the last of the twelve apostles who walked with Jesus would meet with death.

The Roman Emperor stared at the old man. "So you are John, the Apostle of Love," he sneered. "Are you ready to die?"

Before John could answer, an officer approached the Emperor and whispered in his ear, "Perhaps you have heard the saying among the Christians that this John will not die until their God, Jesus, returns."

"Yes, I've heard. In fact, everyone in Rome has heard it!" replied the Emperor. "These Christians are a stubborn and superstitious lot. I will show them! This man will die — today!"

"How shall we kill him?" the officer asked. "Lions don't always kill the Christians, and there have been times the fire did not burn their bodies."

"Cutting off their heads is too noble an end for such as these. That is reserved for Roman citizens," said the Emperor.

The chief executioner spoke up, "What about throwing him in a vat of boiling oil? No one could survive that!"

The emperor nodded his agreement. "Prepare the oil!"

As men rushed to fulfill his order, the herald proclaimed three times, "John the apostle will be boiled in oil." The crowd cheered their approval. They would be witnesses to the death of John the Beloved.

John, one of Jesus' closest friends, was one of the three men Jesus invited into His inner circle. These three, Peter, James, and John, witnessed miracles that the other nine did not. They were the only ones who saw Jesus in all His majesty on the mountaintop, His face shining like the sun and His clothes glowing white as the light.

John was so full of zeal and intensity that Jesus nicknamed him and his brother James, "the sons of thunder." The night Jesus was arrested, John followed the soldiers, entered the high priest's courtyard, and watched to see what would happen to his Lord. Of all the disciples, only John stood boldly with the women at the foot of the cross the day Jesus was crucified.

The Roman Emperor snarled at the apostle. "If your Jesus is really a God, then ask Him to save you!" Then, turning to the executioner, he commanded, "Take him away."

As John waited for the fire to be lit and the oil to boil, he reflected back on other times he had been persecuted for the Gospel. When the paralysed man at the Temple gate was miraculously healed, he and Peter were arrested and imprisoned overnight. The next day they were threatened by the authorities and told, "Never preach again in the name of Jesus."

But all this did was inspire the disciples to pray for more boldness and for more miraculous signs and wonders through the name of Jesus.

A short time later, John was jailed again with several other apostles. This time, they were all released by an angel who told them, "Go and preach in the Temple." They immediately did.

For this, they were beaten by the religious leaders, who again commanded, "Do not preach in the name of Jesus." But the apostles, deciding it was better to obey God than man, kept on preaching. The Lord continued to confirm the Word with signs and wonders.

Since then, John had seen the Lord deliver him time and again. He had survived the persecutions of Nero, which had ended the lives of those who remained of the original twelve disciples.

The gruff voice of a guard brought John back to the present. "Get up, Christian. The oil is ready."

The crowd rose to their feet, clapping and shouting as the prisoner was lowered into the boiling oil. John raised his hands up toward heaven, praying to God.

Minutes passed. John continued to pray.

The cheering of the crowd faded into awed silence. They too had heard it said that this man would never die. Then the whispering started:

"The apostle is not harmed!"

"It's a miracle!"

"His God has protected him! Jesus has protected His apostle!"

The Emperor stared at the apostle in the vat of boiling oil. Against all logic, John was still alive and still praying. The emperor's plan had backfired: Instead of destroying all faith in Jesus Christ, he had actually helped increase it! Frustrated, he looked at the chief executioner, who shrank from under his gaze.

"Is there no way to destroy this man?" the Emperor asked.

But before the executioner could answer, a new cheer from the crowd drew their attention. John was no longer quietly praying; he had started loudly and joyfully worshipping Jesus and celebrating his deliverance from death.

The Emperor made a quick decision. "Get this man out of my sight."

When John was miraculously delivered from the vat of boiling oil, the Emperor gave up trying to kill him. Instead, he banished John to the rocky island of Patmos. For two years, he lived alone in exile. But the Lord was with him and during this time, God revealed to him beautiful scenes and heavenly visions, which he wrote down in the book of Revelation.

When Emperor Domitian died in AD 99, the Roman Senate repealed his judgments and John was released. He was brought back to Ephesus, where he had once been the leader of the church. Even here, he suffered persecution and was forced to drink poison. Yet he remained unharmed, just as Jesus had promised: "If they drink any deadly thing, it shall not hurt them." (See Mark 16:18.)

While in Ephesus, John governed the churches in Asia. He read the gospels of Matthew, Mark, and Luke and verified that they were true. He then wrote the Gospel of John to add his perspective, as well as the three Epistles of John found in the Bible.

John outlived all of the other apostles by more than thirty years. He finally died in peace when he was about 101 years old.

These things I have spoken to you, that in Me you may have peace. In the world you have tribulation, but take courage; I have overcome the world.

Jesus
(JOHN 16:33 NAS)

"Where Is Your Loving Jesus?"

Tsehay Tolessa
Ethiopia
circa 1980s

"They forced my hands under my knees and tied them there. Then they put a stick through these ropes and hung me upside down. They filled my mouth with dirty rags. I almost suffocated. They beat me, breaking my bones. Great pieces of skin hung from my body.

"Then they freed me from bonds and forced me to run with bleeding feet over a path with sharp stones.

"Next, they put me in a small cell containing 62 people. There was only room to stand. Stand on what? On bleeding feet, on broken bones. The cell was completely dark and there was no air. Don't ask how prisoners fulfilled their bodily needs. There was only one hole serving as a toilet, but no one could get to it.

"All had to stand pressed against each other to give a few the opportunity to sleep a bit lying on one side. Because of the limited space, no turning was possible."

Her cuts bled, but there was no medicine. Tsehay could not even hold a cup, so others had to help her drink.

Tsehay Tolessa was tortured by the Ethiopian Communists for her faith in Jesus Christ. She stayed in that cell for over a year, spending a total of ten years in jail. As a result of spending such a long time in darkness, she has not regained full vision.

As they tortured her, the Ethiopian Communists mocked: "Where is your loving Jesus?"

But Tsehay only pitied the blindness of her torturers. She knew that her Lord was always with her, alive in her heart. "Jesus was there, in the midst of human waste, in the humiliation, in the blood and stench. He is more than a King ruling in heaven, a Bridegroom. He is the One tortured in prison."

In all their affliction He was afflicted.

Isaiah 63:9 NAS

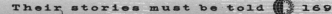

Now I suffer what I suffer; but then Another will be in me who will suffer for me, because I too will be suffering for Him.

Felicitas
Martyred in Carthage, North Africa
AD 202

"His Heart Would Not Die"

Li De Xian
Mainland China
1995

The young evangelist, Li De Xian, filled his backpack with Christian literature preparing to make his weekly trip to Hua Du Village. Over 100 new converts were anxiously awaiting his arrival to begin the home meeting. Within two hours the evangelist arrived, greeted the Christians, and began to deliver his sermon. He showed no sign of fear despite the fact he had been warned that an officer of the Public Security Bureau (PSB) had infiltrated the group and had more than likely informed his superiors of these secret meetings. Although he was not afraid of the authorities, Li was unprepared for what awaited him and the members of this home church.

Li had only been preaching a few minutes when a number of PSB officers charged into the small house and drug him outside. After confiscating all religious materials, the officers noted each attendee and assured them of reprisals. Li was brutally beaten. He was repeatedly kicked in the stomach and groin before the congregation. The young women who were present were grossly molested and loaded into police vans.

Upon arriving at security headquarters, Li was beaten with a heavy club by the superintendent. Seven officers dragged him to an isolation cell, where he was thrown onto the concrete floor and again kicked until he vomited blood. The officers proceeded with their cruelty by alternately beating him on the front and back of his neck. His head was smashed against his knees until he could barely remain conscious. Li was finally beaten in the face with his Bible and left bleeding on the floor.

After seven hours of brutal treatment by the Public Security Bureau, Li was released. Recuperating for only a few weeks, he again travelled to Hua Du Village to encourage the believers. On this trip he was accompanied by Western Christian friends.

Li delivered his message and all seemed to be peaceful until seven security officers stormed the small home and shouted accusations. Upon spotting the foreigners, they quickly departed. Within fifteen minutes a larger number of officers pushed through the gathering and dragged Li outdoors. They began to smash his face against a stone wall. The uniformed officers showed no remorse as they savagely beat the accused. The foreigners began to shout: "Why?" — "What about religious freedom?" — "Why must you beat him?" — "Why?" — "Why?"

The officers turned on the foreigners and they were arrested with Li. The owner of the home was also arrested. She later discovered that it was her son who turned them in.

1998

On May 8, Pastor Li De Xian's church meeting was raided by the police as he preached in the open area in the centre of a village. The authorities confiscated every Bible, songbook, and teaching aid at the service, and then confiscated even the chairs on which the people were sitting.

On May 12, police again raided a house church meeting where Brother Li was preaching. Eighty per cent of the Christians in China regularly attend such illegal house churches. "We told you four days ago not to do this," the policeman shouted. "Don't you know what could happen?"

Li stood in front of his congregation and spoke directly into the loudspeaker for all to hear, "I will preach until I die!"

On June 2, the police were back at one of Brother Li's meetings. This time they carefully photographed the pastor and the members of his congregation, implying that the Christians would be watched. Brother Li was not intimidated. He continued to preach every week and regularly distributed Bibles to members of his flock.

On June 12, an official report about the activities of Pastor Li was sent to the Hua Du Municipal Party Headquarters. Parts of it read:

"Li De Xian is Guangzhou's illegal religious organization's leader Lin Xian Gao's capable and active follower. His career as an illegal religion missionary and he has preached illegally in our town for nearly ten years. He has been arrested and educated many times, and *yet his heart has not died and his nature has not changed....*

"Ten years ago, in the illegal religious gathering spot in Yong Ming Village, there were generally about 150 people who took part in its activities. After these ten years, there are two activities a week in the gathering spot now and each time there are more than 500 people taking part."

(The report also stated that more than a thousand others were gathering to similar meetings in the surrounding villages.)

"If only various units have unified understanding, enhanced education, carry out effective policies, we can then effectively crack down illegal religious activities and create favourable conditions for the stability and development of our town."

On December 1, the PSB again interrupted one of Pastor Li's Tuesday meetings. Without warning, twenty Public Security Bureau (PSB) vehicles swarmed into the neighbourhood, blocking off streets in every direction. No one could come in or go out. It was obvious from such a show of force that they feared there would be a riot. They headed for the illegal house church, just in time for the Tuesday meeting.

Pushing their way into the service, they went straight for Brother Li and seized him. Immediately the police were surrounded by several of the older believers, who clamoured, "Take me instead of Brother Li!" "Let him go. I will go with you!" But that day, no one else was arrested.

As the police led Brother Li to their waiting car, they noticed that he had a bag with him.

"What is that?" they asked,

His calmness amazed the PSB. He was obviously not afraid of going to prison. "It is a blanket and some clothes," Li replied. "I have been expecting you. Three years ago, you told me you were going to take me. I am ready."

As the officers led Brother Li off, the believers began praying blessings over the officers and telling them, "We do not hate you for what you are doing." In the confusion, the officers misunderstood their prayers and thought the believers were putting a curse on them.

"Say that again, and we will throw you into the river," they threatened.

Before things got out of hand, Brother Li turned to the people and told them, "Only pray for me."

Immediately, six hundred people fell to their knees in prayer. The Secretary of the PSB, a high-ranking officer, saw this and was amazed. He asked Li, "How is it that you have so much power? You simply say a word, and the people obey immediately!"

After Li was taken away, the believers went back into the house and finished their meeting. They have continued to meet ever since. Since they have no chairs, they sit on newspapers.

At the police station, the PSB began to interrogate Pastor Li.

But Li had other ideas. "Define my crime," he insisted.

"We do not have to."

Li said, "I do not fear you."

The interrogator hit the table and shouted at Li, "You fear us!"

Li quoted the Bible saying, "The fear of man brings a snare."

Again, the interrogator shouted, "You fear for your life!"

Li said, "Why? You already have me in bonds, what more can you do? Shoot me then — that is all you have left." He went on to quote Matthew 10:28, "Do not fear those who kill the body but cannot kill the soul. But rather fear Him who is able to destroy both soul and body in hell."

The police kept trying to get Li to sign a paper stating he accepted his charges. Li said, "You must be joking. You have not even told me what I am charged with! Name my crime!"

Later on, the Secretary of the PSB shocked Brother Li by admitting to the declining power of Communism. "You have more power than I do," he said. Then he went on to tell Li about how few people came to their Communist Party events, while so many came to Li's meetings. He was amazed at how the believers listened so carefully to everything Li had to say.

During Brother Li's stay in jail, the police shaved his head and placed him in a cell with twelve others. His boldness with the PSB won his cell-mates' admiration, and he was able to share the Gospel with each of them. They told him, "We have noticed something different about you — you really aren't afraid of the PSB."

Li was finally charged with creating public disorder by illegal Gospel preaching and released. Back with his congregation, Brother Li and the believers rejoiced for this chance to share Jesus with the Communist authorities, knowing that when we are persecuted for Jesus' sake, our reward in heaven will be great.

Count yourselves blessed every time people put you down or throw you out or speak lies about you to discredit me. What it means is that the truth is too close for comfort and they are uncomfortable. You can be glad when that happens — give a cheer, even! — for though they don't like it, I do! And all heaven applauds.

Jesus
(MATTHEW 5:11,12 THE MESSAGE)

Don't be upset when they haul you before
the civil authorities. Without knowing it,
they've done you — and me — a favour,
given you a platform for preaching the
kingdom news! And don't worry about
what you'll say or how you'll say it. The
right words will be there; the Spirit of your
Father will supply the words.

Jesus
(MATTHEW 10:17-20 THE MESSAGE)

"A Merry Supper With the Lord"

John Bradford
England
1555

John Bradford stood boldly before the Lord Chancellor. "I urge you," the young man said, "don't condemn the innocent. If you believe I am guilty, you should pass sentence on me. If not, you should set me free."

Bradford, the well-loved pastor of St. Paul's in London, was thrown in prison for his beliefs that differed from the state church during Queen Mary's reign. While in prison, so many of his congregation came to visit him that he continued to preach twice a day. He also preached weekly to the other men in prison, the thieves and common criminals, exhorting them from the Word of God and often giving them money to buy food.

Bradford's keepers trusted him so much, he was often allowed to leave the prison unescorted to visit sick members of his congregation. All he had to do was to promise that he would return by a certain hour. He was so careful about keeping his word that he was usually back well before his curfew.

After a year and a half, Bradford was offered a pardon if he would deny his beliefs, but he would not. Then after six more months in prison, the offer was repeated. Again he refused.

"John," his friends warned, "you need to do something to stall for more time. Ask to discuss your religious beliefs with Queen Mary's learned men. That will take you out of immediate danger."

John replied, "If I did that, the people would think I have begun to doubt the doctrine I confess. I don't doubt it at all."

"Then they will probably kill you very soon," his friends said sadly.

The very next day John was sentenced to death and the keeper's wife came to him with the news: "Tomorrow you will be burned."

Bradford looked to heaven and said, "I thank God for it. I have waited for this for a long time. Lord, make me worthy of this."

Hoping to keep the crowds from knowing what was going on, the guards transferred him to another prison in the middle of the night. But somehow the word got out, and a great multitude came to bid him farewell. Many wept openly as they prayed for him. Bradford, in return, gently said farewell and prayed fervently for them and their future.

At four o'clock the next morning, a large crowd had gathered at the place where Bradford was to be burned. Finally, at nine o'clock, an unusually large number of heavily armed men brought Bradford out to the stake. With him was John Leaf, a teenager, who also refused to deny his faith. Both men fell flat to the ground and prayed for an hour.

Bradford got up, kissed a piece of firewood and then kissed the stake itself. In a loud voice he spoke to the crowd: "England, repent of your sins! Beware of idolatry. Beware of false teachers. See they don't deceive you!" Then he forgave his persecutors and asked the crowd to pray for him.

Turning his head towards John Leaf, he said, "Be of good comfort, brother, for we shall have a merry supper with the Lord tonight!"

Dear friends, don't be surprised at the fiery trials you are going through, as if something strange were happening to you. Instead, be very glad — because these trials will make you partners with Christ in his suffering, and afterward you will have the wonderful joy of sharing his glory when it is displayed to all the world.

Peter the Apostle
Martyred in Rome, AD 65
(1 PETER 4:12,13 NLT)

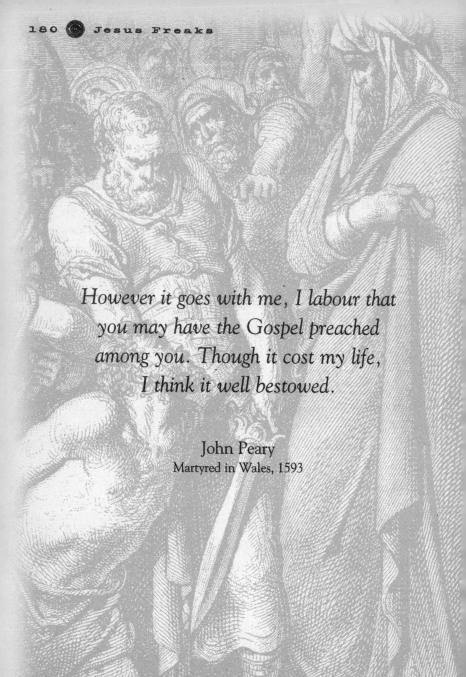

However it goes with me, I labour that
you may have the Gospel preached
among you. Though it cost my life,
I think it well bestowed.

John Peary
Martyred in Wales, 1593

A Decision to Stay

To Dinh Trung
Vietnam
1995

They came without warning, out of nowhere.

Evangelist To Dinh Trung was riding his bike over a rough dirt road in North Vietnam. The ruts in the road demanded his full attention. Suddenly he was surrounded by a squad of Communist police officers who pulled him off his bicycle and started beating him. They made fun of him in front of the crowd of villagers, videotaping everything. Finally, he was taken to prison and kept there without a trial.

Trung had travelled hundreds of miles on his bike while ministering to the K'Ho tribe. Dozens of K'Ho villagers had become Christians after Trung visited them in their homes. But the K'Ho is one of 60 tribes in Vietnam that the government has strictly forbidden Christians to evangelize. Still, a growing number of believers have dedicated themselves to take the good news of the Gospel "outside the camp," where no official churches exist. Some are schoolteachers, more are rice farmers or fishermen. All are persecuted by the Communist government.

Trung was in prison for six months before his trial. He saw this as a divine opportunity to preach to the lost. What else could the Communists do to him? He was already in prison! Through his efforts, many have come to Christ in the prison near Quang Ngai.

Meanwhile, Christians around the world were alerted to Trung's situation. Many prayed and wrote letters on his behalf. Because of the pressure put on Vietnamese authorities, Trung was offered an early release. The only problem: The evangelist wasn't ready to leave! He felt God's call to stay in prison and disciple his new flock of believers. Trung refused his early release and chose to serve his full sentence.

Trung was greatly encouraged when he heard of the many letters written by Christians on his behalf. He knows he is called to be an evangelist in Vietnam — which is a very dangerous occupation. The prayers and letters gave him the strength to continue to be a witness to his fellow inmates for the kingdom of God.

"I don't care about my own life. The most important thing is that I complete my mission, the work that the Lord Jesus gave me — to tell people the good news about God's grace."

My life is worth nothing unless I use it for doing the work assigned me by the Lord Jesus — the work of telling others the Good News about God's wonderful kindness and love.

Paul the Apostle
Martyred in Rome, AD 65
(ACTS 20:24 NLT)

For we do not want you to be unaware,
brethren, of our affliction which came to
us in Asia, that we were burdened
excessively, beyond our strength, so that
we despaired even of life;

indeed, we had the sentence of death
within ourselves in order that we should
not trust in ourselves, but in God who
raises the dead;

who delivered us from so great a peril of
death, and will deliver us....

you also joining in helping us through your
prayers, that thanks may be given by
many persons on our behalf for the favour
bestowed upon us through the
prayers of many.

Paul the Apostle
Martyred in Rome, AD 65
(2 CORINTHIANS 1:8-11 NAS)

In the Dog Pit

Trofim Dimitrov
Belene, Bulgaria
1960s

Trofim Dimitrov could hear the dogs barking long before he reached the pit. On the way, he prayed fervently for his enemies, the guards, who then threw him down, naked, to the hungry dogs.

Immediately, a great howling was heard.

When the officers looked into the pit, they saw Brother Dimitrov kneeling in prayer and the dogs in panic. Barking wildly, the dogs were trying to jump the walls in order to save themselves from the strange power emanating from him!

Let all who take refuge in you be glad; let them ever sing for joy. Spread your protection over them, that those who love your name may rejoice in you.

For surely, O LORD, you bless the righteous; you surround them with your favour as with a shield.

Psalm 5:11,12 NIV

A Communist officer told a Christian he was beating, "I am almighty, as you suppose your God to be. I can kill you."

The Christian answered, "The power is all on my side. I can love you while you torture me to death."

Stopped by Terrorists

Romulo Sauñe
Peru
1992

The terrorists stood in front of the roadblock waving their guns at the motorists. "Get out of your car and form a single line," one of them ordered. Pastor Romulo Sauñe and three friends — all Christian workers — had been driving back from a church party and were in a festive mood. Now, they quickly obeyed the terrorist's instructions and stood in line with the other passengers.

Sauñe quickly sized up the situation. Five buses had been burned and six bodies lay on the ground, murdered by the Senderistas, a Marxist group in Peru. As he stood waiting, he felt the compassion of God for the Senderistas and decided to present the Gospel to them. He boldly told them, "God loves you and I love you. There is no sin that cannot be forgiven. Even now, God is willing to forgive your sins because He loves you. The blood of the Lord Jesus can clean and purify your souls."

At first, the Senderistas listened very attentively as the Gospel was presented. Then they were interrupted by another terrorist, who seemed to be the leader of the group. Waving his gun, he told the four Christians, "You are guilty of fooling the people with your religion. Today, you are being judged."

Without any more words, the terrorist leader opened fire. The bodies of the four martyrs fell — first on their knees as if they were praying to God and then to the ground. The witnesses of this massacre testified that Pastor Romulo died saying, "God, I love You! Jesus, I love You!"

Romulo Sauñe was well-known among Christians for his translation of the Holy Bible into Quechua–Ayacucho, the language of his people. For many years, he had laboured to complete this massive work, travelling to Lima, Peru, as well as to the United States.

A short time before the massacre, Pastor Romulo had returned to Chakiqpampa, Peru, his birthplace, to celebrate the anniversary of the church where his grandfather, Pastor Justiniano Quicaña, had been assassinated by the Senderistas in December 1989.

The church anniversary was held with great rejoicing. Pastor Romulo had brought Bibles, New Testaments, food, and a great quantity of clothes to distribute to the needy of the city. As he preached the Word on his last day of life, thirteen men and fifteen women gave their lives to the Lord Jesus.

The day after the massacre, as a procession carried the bodies of the martyrs to the cemetery, other believers fearlessly joined them in a Christian victory march, demonstrating that, as Christians, they too were ready to give their lives for the love of the Lord Jesus Christ.

Romulo Sauñe knew he had an assignment from God — to translate the Bible into Quechua–Ayacucho, the native tongue of his people. Many are now able to read the Word of God for themselves — and will come to a

saving faith in the Lord Jesus — because of his obedience.
His life made a difference!

*If any of you want to be my followers, you must forget
about yourself. You must take up your cross and follow
me. If you want to save your life, you will destroy it. But
if you give up your life for me and for the good news, you
will save it... Don't be ashamed of me and my message
among these unfaithful and sinful people! If you are, the
Son of Man will be ashamed of you when he comes in the
glory of his Father with the holy angels.*

Jesus

(MARK 8:34,35,38 CEV)

I'd Rather Be in Prison

Gao Feng
Mainland China
circa 1997

Seven Chinese guards surrounded Gao Feng, who was handcuffed to a chair. The guards took turns shocking him with cattle prods. "Eat!" they commanded. "And we will stop."

Feng had gone on a hunger strike to get back his copy of the Scriptures which the guards had taken from him. They were torturing him to get him to stop the hunger strike. At times, he thought he could no longer stand the pain, but he didn't give up. They never broke his spirit.

"You couldn't reason with the guards," Feng said, "because they weren't human."

Gao Feng, a 30-year-old worker at Chrysler's Jeep plant in Beijing, had tried to work within the Communist government system to get a Protestant church registered. Only government-sanctioned churches are legal in China. All others are illegal, their services are often disrupted by the police, and the pastors and congregations are beaten and imprisoned.

Feng collected signatures for a petition seeking government registration for his church so they could meet legally. For this "crime" he was arrested and sent to prison without a trial, his home and possessions confiscated.

As a result of his hunger strike, Feng was sent to a northern province for "re-education through labour." While there, he lived in a 12-by-20-foot cell with sixteen other prisoners. They spent twelve hours each day working in the fields. At night, with so many in such a small cell, they had to arrange themselves a certain way so that everyone could lay down.

When he was transferred back to Beijing, he refused to chant the pro-government slogans with the other prisoners, so his "re-education" was continued. This time, his brainwashing included being forced to watch the news every evening on government-controlled TV. Finally, after more than two years in prison and in re-education camps, Feng was released on February 7, 1998.

To Feng, it was all worth it, and he would happily go to prison again. "I would prefer to be in prison for two years than to do nothing for God," he said. In fact, he feels lucky. As news of his situation reached believers in many countries, people wrote to the Chinese government demanding his release. Feng says the international attention focused on his case earned him better treatment from the Chinese authorities. "Others who are less well-known are simply executed."

Watch for news of Christians who are held prisoners for their faith. Look up their countries in the back of this book and see how you can pray for them. Write letters. It makes a difference!

> *Open your mouth for the speechless,*
> *In the cause of all who are appointed to die.*
> *Open your mouth, judge righteously;*
> *And plead the cause of the poor and needy.*
>
> Proverbs 31:8,9 NKJV

Now I Am Strong

Thomas Hudson
England
1558

The crowd looked on, curious about what the martyr would do next. Thomas Hudson had come this far without denying his faith. The bishop had questioned him again and again, he'd not weakened in prison, and now he was walking to the place of execution. At the last minute, would he recant?

Just before the chain around him was made fast, Hudson stooped, slipped out from under the chain, and stood a little to one side. A hush came over the crowd — everyone wondered why he hesitated. The Christians prayed.

Only Hudson knew the real reason he had stepped down. At the last minute he had suddenly been attacked with doubts and felt his faith growing weak. Not willing to die while feeling this way, he fell upon his knees and prayed to God, who sent him comfort.

Then he rose with great joy, as a reborn man, and cried, "Now, thank God, I am strong. I don't care what man can do to me!"

Going to the stake again, he put the chain around himself.

The fire was lit.

Finally, let the mighty strength of the Lord make you strong. Put on all the armor that God gives, so you can defend yourself against the devil's tricks. We are not fighting against humans. We are fighting against forces and authorities and against rulers of darkness and powers in the spiritual world. So put on all the armor that God gives. Then when that evil day comes, you will be able to defend yourself. And when the battle is over, you will still be standing firm.

Paul the Apostle
Martyred in Rome, AD 65
(EPHESIANS 6:10-13 CEV)

"You Will Indeed Drink From My Cup"

James, Son of Zebedee
Jerusalem, Israel
AD 44

"James, John, come with me!" James and his brother, John, followed their mother, who knelt at Jesus' feet. "Lord, will You do a favour for me?" she asked.

"What would you like Me to do?" Jesus asked.

Their mother said, "Grant that one of my two sons may sit at Your right and the other at Your left in Your kingdom."

"You don't know what you are asking," Jesus said. Then He turned to the two men. "Can you drink the cup I am going to drink?"

"We can," James and John answered together.

Jesus said to them, "You will indeed drink from My cup."

Several years later, King Herod Agrippa decided to stop the spread of Christianity by striking its leaders. He had James arrested and sentenced to death on the basis of one man's testimony. However, when this accuser saw James' extraordinary courage and steadfast joy, even when condemned to die, the man was deeply touched in his heart. There on the spot, the accuser made a decision for Christ. He boldly cried out, "I want to follow Jesus also. I am a Christian."

The soldiers led James to be executed. Along the way, his accuser stopped the apostle and fell down at his feet. "I am so sorry for what I have done," he cried. "The blood of an innocent man is on my hands. Please, please, before you die, please forgive me."

James paused for a moment, then said, "Peace be to you, brother," and gave him a holy kiss.

Then the man said, "You should not receive the crown of martyrdom alone. I will die with you." He was immediately sentenced to death and they were both brought to the place of execution.

Minutes later, the two were beheaded together.

Just as Jesus had foretold, James, the son of Zebedee, was martyred, the first of the twelve disciples to die for his faith.

Raising his eyes in prayer, [Jesus] said....

"I spelled out your character in detail
To the men and women you gave me.
They were yours in the first place;
Then you gave them to me...
Everything mine is yours, and yours mine,
And my life is on display in them.
For I'm no longer going to be visible in the world:
They'll continue in the world
While I return to you.
Holy Father, guard them as they pursue this life

That you conferred as a gift through me,

So they can be one heart and mind

As we are one heart and mind."

Jesus
(JOHN 17:1,6,10,11 THE MESSAGE)

"I Always Have Jesus Before My Eyes"

John Stanescu
Romania
1960s

The Russian colonel entered the cell carrying the cane used for beating prisoners. As director of the slave labour camp, he had been informed that someone had dared to preach the Gospel. "Who is the culprit?" he demanded. When no one responded, he said, "Well, then *all* will be flogged."

He started at one end of the cell. Soon the air was filled with the usual yelling and tears. When he came to Stanescu, he said, "Not ready yet? Strip this minute!"

As he stood up, the Romanian deacon John Stanescu replied, "There is a God in heaven, and He will judge you." With this, John's fate was sealed. Everyone knew he would surely be beaten to death. There was a sudden hush.

At that moment, a guard entered saying, "Colonel Albon, you are called urgently to the office. Some high-ranking generals have come from the Ministry."

The colonel left, saying to Stanescu, "We will see each other again soon."

However, things did not turn out as the colonel had planned. Communists hate and often jail each other for no reason, and the generals had come that day to arrest the colonel! After an hour, Colonel Albon was back in the cell, this time as a prisoner.

Many inmates jumped at him to lynch him. But Stanescu jumped to his defence, shielding the defeated enemy with his own body. He received many blows himself as he protected the torturer from the flogged prisoners. Stanescu was a real priest, a royal priest.

A Christian prisoner later asked him, "Where did you get the power to do this?"

He replied, "I love Jesus ardently. I always have Him before my eyes. I also see Him in my enemy. It is Jesus who keeps them from doing even worse things.

"The grace of God brings about His blessings in the spiritual and the material realms. As His children, we do not have to be buffeted about by all the torments that afflict the world. Even when trouble comes, the sunlight of God is shining, and there is peace within us."

I've got my eye on the goal, where God is beckoning us onward — to Jesus. I'm off and running, and I'm not turning back.

So let's keep focused on that goal, those of us who want everything God has for us. If any of you have something else in mind, something less than total commitment, God will clear your blurred vision — you'll see it yet!

Paul the Apostle
Martyred in Rome, AD 65
(PHILIPPIANS 3:13-15 THE MESSAGE)

The church has an unconditional obligation to the victims of any ordering of society. There are things for which an uncompromising stand is worthwhile.

Dietrich Bonhoeffer
Hanged in Germany for resisting the Nazis
1945

A Night Swim

Brother Barout
Laos
1975

"One hundred soldiers with machine guns circled the few acres surrounding the Lao Biblical Training School. It was 1975, the year the Communists conquered Laos. Along with the other sixty students and our teachers, I was held in a small room for two weeks while we were interrogated. One by one, we were called before the soldiers who tried to get us to denounce Christ. We had little food and ate grass out in the school yard.

"The Communist army then brought three hundred government students to scream at us in an organized 'demonstration of the people.' These government students surrounded our school shouting, 'Everything belongs to the government! Your pigs and fish are ours!' The soldiers then took all the animals that the Bible school had been using for food.

"Finally, the soldiers gave up trying to convert us to follow Marx and Lenin, the founders of Communism. Most of us were allowed to go home after two weeks."

But Brother Barout chose not to go home.

"On the Sunday morning we were released, I decided to escape to Thailand to have more freedom to share Christ. Thousands of Laotian refugees who had fled from the Communists lived in camps in Thailand, just across the Mekong River. There were only three Christians among them.

"Another Bible student decided to come with me. We could not say good-bye to our families. First, there was no time; and second, we could not trust them since they were not Christians. The government had turned families against each other.

"The Mekong River is very wide, and that winter was the coldest we had seen. I was also sick with a fever and thought I might die. Standing in the bush on the edge of the water, I asked my Christian friend, 'How can we go?'

"He replied courageously, 'We are Christians. We will go to heaven if we drown. If we die, we die together.'

"At 10:00 p.m. we entered the cold, muddy river. We both had Bibles in large plastic bags tied on our backs. I thought, 'Lord, if we die, at least when they find our Bibles, they will know that we are Christians.'

"We were swimming only fifty yards from one of the guard towers on shore. My friend was so cold that he was shaking. When he shifted his plastic bag to his chest to try to float on top of it, I told him to get off or they would see him. He splashed a little as he got back down in the water, so a spotlight came over from the shore to where the bag had splashed. We heard the guards say, 'Oh, a big fish.'

"Finally, in the darkness, we climbed up on the muddy river bank in Thailand. Looking at our waterproof watches we saw that our swim had taken 48 minutes. We were free and continued to serve the Lord."

Today Laos still is not free. A few churches are officially open in Vientiane (the capital), but nowhere else.

Three out of four of those are considered subversive to the government and are watched. The police are very strict. Recently, when a Christian man helped to feed some poor villagers, he told them of an open church in the capital. Thirty-five of the villagers went to visit the church and thirty of them gladly received Jesus. When they returned to their village, the authorities took away their jobs.

Pray for new believers in all countries, that God will strengthen them by the Word that is in their hearts and will help them to withstand persecution. Pray for strength for those who would risk their lives to take the Gospel to people who have yet to hear it. Pray for their protection and that their efforts will reap new souls.

Jubilant Dance for Jesus

Russian Captain
Romania
1940s

"Christianity has become dramatic with us," wrote Pastor Richard Wurmbrand, a leader of the underground church in Communist Romania. "When Christians in free countries win a soul for Christ, the new believer may become a member of a quietly living church. But when those in captive nations win someone, we know that he may have to go to prison and that his children may become orphans. The joy of having brought someone to Christ is always mixed with this feeling that there is a price that must be paid.

"When I was still living behind the Iron Curtain, I had met a Russian captain. He loved God, he longed after God, but he had never seen a Bible. He had never attended religious services. He had no religious education, but he loved God without the slightest knowledge of Him.

"I read to him the Sermon on the Mount and the parables of Jesus. After hearing them, he danced around the room in rapturous joy, proclaiming, 'What a wonderful beauty! How could I live without knowing this Christ?' It was the first time that I saw someone jubilating in Christ.

"Then I made a mistake. I read to him the passion and crucifixion of Christ, without having prepared him for this. He had not expected it. When he heard how Christ was beaten, how He was crucified, and that in the end He died, he fell in an armchair and began to weep bitterly. He had believed in a Saviour and now his Saviour was dead!

"I looked at him and was ashamed that I had called myself a Christian and a pastor, a teacher of others. I had never shared the sufferings of Christ as this Russian officer now shared them. Looking at him was, for me, like seeing Mary Magdalene weeping at the foot of the cross or at the empty tomb.

"Then I read to him the story of the resurrection. When he heard this wonderful news, that the Saviour arose from the tomb, he slapped his knees, and shouted for joy: 'He is alive! He is alive!' Again he danced around the room, overwhelmed with happiness!

"I said to him, 'Let us pray!'

"He fell on his knees together with me. He did not know our holy phrases. His words of prayer were, 'O God, what a fine chap You are! If I were You and You were me, I would never have forgiven You Your sins. But You are really a very nice chap! I love You with all my heart.'

"I think that all the angels in heaven stopped what they were doing to listen to this sublime prayer from this Russian officer. When this man received Christ, he knew he would immediately lose his position as an officer, that prison and perhaps death in jail would almost surely follow. He gladly paid the price. He was ready to lose everything."

Though you have not seen him, you love him; and even though you do not see him now, you believe in him

and are filled with an inexpressible and glorious joy, for you are receiving the goal of your faith, the salvation of your souls.

Peter the Apostle
Martyred in Rome, AD 65
(1 PETER 1:8,9 NIV)

I Won't Bow Down!

Bartholomew
Armenia
AD 70

"You are unsettling the worship of our gods. And not only that, you have perverted my own brother!" the king of Armenia shouted at Bartholomew. But Bartholomew did not back down.

One of the original twelve disciples, he had boldly preached Jesus Christ for 37 years. Starting in the heathen cities throughout what is now Turkey, he then travelled to India. Here, after he learned the language, he translated the gospel of Matthew and taught the Indians in their native tongue. Later he preached in twelve different cities in the country of Armenia (located between the present-day countries of Turkey and Iran). Many people turned from idolatry to worship Jesus, including the king of Armenia's brother and his family.

Bartholomew boldly answered the king, saying, "I have preached the true worship of God throughout your country. I have not *perverted* your brother and his family, but rather have *converted* them to the truth."

King Astyages threatened Bartholomew, "Unless you stop preaching Christ and make sacrifices to the god Ashtaroth, you will be put to death."

"You can be sure of this, King Astyages, I will never sacrifice to your idol. I would rather seal my testimony with my blood than do the smallest act against my faith or conscience."

Upon hearing this, the king ordered, "I want this man to suffer severe torture. First, beat him with rods. After that, suspend him upside down on a cross and skin him alive!"

Following the king's command, Bartholomew was beaten, crucified, and flayed. Despite all this, he was still conscious and continued to exhort the people to believe in Jesus and worship the true God.

Finally, to prevent him from saying anything else, the king's men took an axe and cut off his head. Bartholomew was united with Jesus, his Lord.

Throughout history, Jesus Freaks like Bartholomew have remained at their sacred tasks until their voices were silenced by death. They kept on in their witness, hoping that their last few words would help yet one more person believe.

We work hard and suffer much in order that people will believe the truth, for our hope is in the living God, who is the Saviour of all people.

Paul the Apostle
Martyred in Rome, AD 65
(1 TIMOTHY 4:10 NLT)

Sufferings gladly borne for others convert more people than sermons.

Therese of Lisieux

Writing With Soap

Xu Yonghai
Mainland China
1995

Xu Yonghai looked around his 8-by-8-foot cell. A trained medical doctor, Yonghai was used to sanitized conditions — so what he saw was especially disgusting. There was no bathroom. Instead, there was a pipe in one corner from which water flowed continuously onto the concrete. Yonghai learned to use this pipe to wash human waste from his cell. He ate right there as well — guards slid his food under the door. He drank and washed himself with water from the pipe.

For two entire years, he never once left this tiny, filthy room!

Yonghai, a Christian in Communist China, had worked with Gao Feng to get a house church legalized. For this "crime," he was locked up in a Beijing prison for 24 months. Yonghai spent much of this time in prayer and meditation — and writing. On the walls of his cell, Yonghai scrawled the major points for a book, *God the Creator*. He wrote with soap, his deep-thinking, intellectual mind tying the points of his thesis together. When the writing was finished, he spent time memorizing the words. After his release in May 1997, he put his cell-wall composition on paper. The result was a 50,000-word book!

"My cell was the last stop for prisoners sentenced to die," Yonghai said. "At times there were as many as three other prisoners in the tiny, damp room, awaiting their date with the executioner."

What a chance to witness! What an opportunity to introduce these men into God's kingdom! Yonghai took advantage of it, sharing the Gospel with his temporary cell mates in their final days on earth. He reports, "These men were very open to the message of Christ."

"My living conditions were disgusting, but after four months, the Lord helped me get used to it. God was with me, even in my darkest times, helping me endure my years in prison. Only God gave me the strength to do it."

You are My servant, I have chosen you and have not cast you away: Fear not, for I am with you; Be not dismayed, for I am your God. I will strengthen you, Yes, I will help you, I will uphold you with My righteous right hand.

Isaiah 41:9,10 NKJV

A Ploughman's Bible

William Tyndale
Belgium
1536

"It would be wrong to translate God's holy Word into English," the Doctor of Divinity said sternly. "Only a language like Latin or Greek is able to fully convey God's truth. English is a vulgar language — fine for ploughmen and shopkeepers, but hardly suitable for the Bible."

William Tyndale's eyes blazed. He was a highly educated man, fluent in several languages, including Greek and Hebrew. "Not only *can* an accurate English translation be done, it *should* be done. The Scriptures of God are being hidden from the people's eyes. The only way that poor people can read and see the simple, plain Word of God is if it is turned into their mother tongue, English."

In the early 1500s, only scholars could read God's Word. The only legal Bible was in Latin, which most of the common people could not understand. Since they could not read God's Word for themselves, they had to rely upon what others told them it said.

It was illegal to own an English Bible or even memorize Scripture in English. In fact, in 1519, seven Christians were burned at the stake in Coventry, England, for teaching their children the Lord's Prayer and the Ten Commandments in English!

Before long, the two men were arguing heatedly. Tyndale quoted Scriptures, the doctor quoted man-made traditions and church rules. Finally, the Doctor of Divinity shouted, "It would be better to be without God's laws than without the Pope's."

Tyndale courageously replied, "I defy the Pope and all his laws! In fact, if God spares my life, I intend to make it possible for a common farmer, a ploughman, to know more of the Scripture than you do!"

Within a year of Tyndale's conversation with the Doctor of Divinity, he decided it was no longer safe for him to stay in England, so he travelled to Germany. There he lived under an assumed name while he worked to finish his translation. When spies from England found him in Germany, he escaped to Belgium, where he printed thousands of his New Testaments.

In 1526, Tyndale's English New Testament began trickling into England. The Scriptures, now referred to as the "pirate edition," were made smaller than conventional books. This size was easier to smuggle into bales of cotton and containers of wheat being shipped into England.

As copies poured into England, they were eagerly bought and read by all sorts of ordinary people, who often sat up all night reading them or hearing them read. When the Bishop of London discovered the New Testaments, he bought as many as he could on the black market, paying full price for them. He declared, "I intend to burn and destroy them all." The merchant who had smuggled them into England gave the money to Tyndale, who then printed three times as many in a revised version. The Bishop of London had unknowingly become Tyndale's foremost financial supporter!

When Tyndale heard the Bibles were thrown into the fire, he said, "I expected they would burn the New Testaments. I expect they want to burn me too! This may yet happen, if it is God's will. Even so, I know I did my duty in translating the New Testament."

Within the next ten years, Tyndale's New Testament was widely distributed throughout England. Bible truths were now available to everyone, and many people discovered they could have a personal relationship with God based on His Word. At the same time, anyone caught with this illegal book faced severe persecution. Prisons were overflowing and thousands of Christians were executed. Weekly, reports of the persecutions would come to Tyndale, who remained in exile in Europe and continued his translation of the Old Testament. Two of Tyndale's close friends were burned at the stake. Even church officials, once persecutors, became martyrs after finding truth in Tyndale's work.

In the spring of 1535, a man named Henry Phillips arrived in Antwerp, where Tyndale had been hiding. In hopes of a reward, Phillips took it on himself to betray Tyndale. He befriended Tyndale, noting that he was "simple and inexpert in the wily subtleties of this world." Before Tyndale knew what was happening, Phillips had set an ambush for him.

Tyndale spent the next eighteen months in prison near Brussels, Belgium. With the help of Miles Coverdale, he was able to complete part of the Old Testament. During his stay in prison, his powerful preaching and the sincerity of his life greatly influenced those around him. The jailer, the jailer's daughter, and others of his household accepted the Lord Jesus as their personal Saviour.

On October 6, 1536, Tyndale was taken from his dungeon and strangled. Then his body was burned. His last words were a fervent prayer: "Lord, open the King of England's eyes!"

God honoured Tyndale's prayer. Within three years, the King of England gave instructions that a copy of the "Great Bible" completed by Tyndale's co-worker, Coverdale, including Tyndale's New Testament be placed in every church in England!

Tyndale's translation was so accurate that 75 years later, when the *King James Version* of the Bible was published, it was based largely upon Tyndale's work. In fact, about 90 percent of the words remain exactly as he wrote them!

Many people today don't know that countless martyrs shed their blood to make God's Word available in English. Having the Scriptures available in the language of common people challenged the established church to return to its scriptural origins and to rediscover the truth and power of a personal relationship with God through Jesus Christ.

What if these courageous men and women had not taken a stand for making God's Word available to everyone? Would we be Christians today?

I never knew all there was in the Bible until I spent those years in jail. I was constantly finding new treasures.

John Bunyan
Imprisoned for a total of 12 years
England
1660s and 1670s

People need more than bread for their life;

they must feed on every word of God.

Jesus
(MATTHEW 4:4 NLT)

"Suffering Did Not Diminish My Faith"

Mizhong Miao
Mainland China
During the Red Guard Era, 1966–1969

"Abandon your faith!" the Communist police officer shouted at Mizhong Miao. The officer's fist slammed down on the table.

Miao replied quietly, "Jesus is the Saviour of my life. I cannot obey your order."

Only seven weeks after his conversion from atheism, Mizhong Miao became a preacher of the Gospel. This is a common occurrence in underground churches in China. Believers there don't wait for theological studies, but begin right away to tell about their first experiences with Jesus.

Miao had been arrested for spreading what the police called "the poison of imperialism." They beat him — and he prayed. While they beat him, a supernatural joy filled him. He felt the Holy Spirit surround him, and nothing the Communists did could make him deny Jesus. He was sentenced to five years, but was later given another ten years for preaching in the slave labour camp.

Miao's wife, abandoning all hope of ever seeing him again, divorced him. When he heard the news, he was very sad. Then he remembered these words from Psalm 73:25 NKJV: "Whom have I in heaven but You? And there is none upon earth that I desire besides You." He composed a hymn and sang it.

Miao continued to preach to his fellow inmates. Then came a terrible winter, with temperatures close to zero. An epidemic swept through the prison. Out of 1,300 prisoners, 1,050 died. Miao was pronounced dead and taken to the morgue, but his spirit was alive. In the morgue, surrounded by dead men, he prayed and saw an angel, dressed in white, whose face shone with God's glory. The angel blew upon him. Immediately the sickness left him, and he felt better. He knelt and thanked God, then he left the morgue.

The prison doctor saw him walking around and cried out in fear. He thought Miao was a ghost, just like the disciples did when the resurrected Jesus appeared to them. But Miao said, "Don't be afraid. I am Mizhong Miao. God restored me to health. He sent me to show you the way to God." The doctor knelt and said, "Your God is a reality."

After fifteen years, Miao was released from prison and continued to work secretly in the underground church for another eighteen years. At his release, he told the authorities, "Suffering did not diminish my faith but only intensified my relationship with Jesus."

It has been said, "A man with an argument is no match for a man with an experience."

Jesus Freaks have a radical relationship with Jesus. They have experienced His touch on their lives — and they will never forget it.

We Will Die With You

Philip, Matthew, Jude,
and Simon the Zealot
Roman Empire
AD 33

"But Teacher," said one of the twelve solemn men, "the last time You were in Jerusalem, the Jews tried to stone You."

Another spoke up, "It wasn't that long ago, either. Are You *sure* You want to go back there?"

Jesus' answer only made them more confused. Why was He talking about walking in the daylight and stumbling at night? Finally Jesus said plainly, "Lazarus is dead. And for your sakes, I am glad I wasn't there, because this will give you another opportunity to believe in Me. Come, let us go to him."

Then Thomas turned to the rest of the disciples and said, "Let's go too. We might as well die with Him." They agreed, and all went to Jerusalem with Jesus.

As it turned out, no one died. Instead, Lazarus was miraculously raised from the dead in front of many witnesses. But from then on the religious leaders plotted to kill Jesus.

The night before His arrest, as Jesus and His disciples approached the Mount of Olives, Jesus told them, "Tonight you will all desert Me, for it is written: 'I will strike the shepherd, and the sheep of the flock will be scattered.' But after I have risen, I will go ahead of you into Galilee."

Peter replied, "Even if everyone else deserts you, I never will."

Jesus answered, "This very night, before the cock crows, you will deny you know Me three times."

But Peter insisted, "Even if I have to die with You, I will never deny You." And all the other disciples said the same thing.

That night, when the soldiers came to arrest Jesus, all of the disciples ran off just as Jesus had predicted. Later, Peter and John watched the Lord's trial from the safety of the dark courtyard. Only John joined the women at the foot of the cross.

It wasn't until after the Resurrection and the Day of Pentecost that the disciples became bold witnesses for the Lord. They knew Jesus was the true Messiah, the Son of the Living God. They had heard His words, had seen His miracles, and had witnessed His resurrection. Persecutions, threats, beatings, imprisonment, even the death of their friends and fellow believers could not silence them.

Not one of them quit and went back to the family business. Instead, these few men single-handedly took the Gospel story throughout the known world. In the end, all faced death for their Lord rather than deny Him again.

Philip

Right after Stephen was martyred in AD 34, Philip travelled to Samaria, where he led an early revival that was accompanied by signs and great miracles. Later, when the disciples divided the known world between them, Philip drew what is now Turkey and Syria. He taught and planted churches in many cities in this region.

Finally, he came to Hierapolis in Phrygia. The idol worshippers there would not listen to the Gospel Philip preached, even though the Lord worked several miraculous signs in their city. Some ancient historians say they whipped him, threw him in prison, and later crucified him. Other historians say he was tied to a pillar and stoned to death.

Philip died in AD 51, becoming the second apostle to be martyred.

Matthew

While still in Jerusalem, Matthew wrote his gospel to the Jews in Hebrew. Later, at the dividing of the countries among the disciples, Matthew drew Ethiopia. There, he accomplished much, with teaching as well as with miracles.

Ethiopia's King Aeglippus favoured the Christians, but when he died, an unbelieving heathen took the throne. King Hytacus had Matthew arrested while he stood teaching in his church. He was dragged outside, nailed to the ground with short spears, and beheaded. He died in AD 66.

Jude, Brother of James

Jude, also known as Thaddaeus and Lebbaeus, wrote the book of Jude. He was also the younger brother of Jesus and James the Less. He travelled in Mesopotamia, Syria, Arabia, and Persia (present-day Iran), reaching as far as Edema. There, he preached boldly against worshipping idols and making heathen sacrifices. When the pagan priests saw that they were losing followers — and money — because of Jude's teaching, they attacked him with sticks and clubs, beating him to death. He died in AD 68.

Simon the Zealot

Simon the Zealot was also known as Simon the Canaanite. He preached the Gospel in Egypt, North Africa, Mauritania (an island in the Indian Ocean), and in the islands of Great Britain. Some historians say he was crucified in Great Britain in AD 70.

Other historians say Simon left Great Britain and went to Persia, where he found Jude. Together they steadfastly continued teaching and preaching until Jude's death in AD 68. Later that same year, Simon was painfully tortured and crucified by a governor in Syria.

A servant is not greater than the master. Since they persecuted me, naturally they will persecute you. And if they had listened to me, they would listen to you! The people of the world will hate you because you belong to me, for they don't know God who sent me.

Jesus
(JOHN 15:20,21 NLT)

Honour Your Mother

Fang-Cheng
Mainland China
1950s

"Tell us!" the officer shouted, as he brought the whip down again across the pastor's back. "We must know who else is working with you." Day after day, the Chinese Communists tortured Rev. Fang-Cheng, but no matter what they did to him, he steadfastly refused to give them the names of his fellow Christians.

One day Cheng was brought again before the examining officer. In a corner of the room, he saw a heap of rags and heard a rattling of chains. As the image became clearer, he realized it was his mother. Before she did not have white hair; now she had. The colour of her face was like ashes. He could see that she too had passed through heavy suffering.

The Communist spoke to Cheng: "I have heard that you Christians have Ten Commandments, supposedly given by God, which you strive to obey. I would be interested in knowing them. Would you be so kind as to recite the Ten Commandments?"

Cheng was in a terrible state of heart, but any opportunity to acquaint a Communist with God's law must not be neglected. He began to list the commandments. When he arrived at "Honour your father and mother," he was interrupted.

The Communist told him, "Cheng, I wish to give you the opportunity to honour your mother. Here she is, suffering in chains. Tell us what you know about your brethren in faith and I promise that tonight you and your mother will be free. You will be able to give her care and honour. Let me see now whether you really believe in God and wish to fulfil His commandment."

It was not easy to make a decision. Cheng turned to his mother: "Mother, what shall I do?"

The mother answered, "I have taught you from childhood to love Christ and His holy Church. Don't mind my suffering. Seek to remain faithful to the Saviour and His little brothers. If you betray, you are no more my son."

This was the last time that Fang-Cheng saw his mother. It was likely that she died under torture.

No test or temptation that comes your way is beyond the course of what others have had to face. All you need to remember is that God will never let you down; he'll never let you be pushed past your limit; he'll always be there to help you come through it.

Paul the Apostle
Beheaded in Rome, AD 65
(1 CORINTHIANS 10:13 THE MESSAGE)

My Lord was pleased to die for my sins;
why should I not be glad to give up my
poor life out of love to Him.

Girolamo Savanarola
Martyred, Florence, Italy
1498

The Happiest Day

Nijole Sadunaite
Soviet Lithuania
1970s

When Nijole Sadunaite was sentenced in Soviet Lithuania, she told the court:

"This is the happiest day of my life. I was judged today for the cause of truth and love toward men. What cause could be more important? I have an enviable fate, a glorious destiny. My condemnation will be my triumph. I regret only having done so little for men.

"Standing today on the side of the eternal truth of Jesus Christ, I remember His fourth beatitude: 'Blessed are they which do hunger and thirst after righteousness, for they shall be filled.' There exists no greater joy than to suffer for truth and for one's fellow men. How could I not rejoice when God Almighty has promised that light will overcome darkness and truth will overcome error and lies!

"We must condemn evil, but we must love the man, even the one in error. This you can learn only at the school of Jesus Christ, who is the only truth for all, the only way, and the only life. Good Jesus, Your kingdom comes into our souls."

She was sentenced to three years in prison.

After being freed, she met the Pope in Rome, and he asked her, "How was it in jail?"

She replied, "Romantic."

Words pronounced by martyrs before the authorities are not human words, the simple expression of a human conviction, but words pronounced by the Holy Spirit through the confessors of faith.

Thomas Aquinas

Extreme Love

Jackie Hamill and Juliet
Philippines
1992

The service was over. Jackie Hamill, a young Australian prison evangelist, was excited about what God was doing. She had felt the love of Jesus reach out to these inmates. Jackie and fourteen members of her church had travelled to the Philippines to minister in a military prison there. They were concerned for the lost souls of the inmates, many of whom were Communist guerrillas in prison for murder.

Suddenly, the quiet was broken by the sounds of fighting and gunshots. The inmates were rioting and had overpowered the guards, seizing their guns and ammunition to make an escape.

The evangelists were taken hostage and held for three days. During this time, Jackie and one other girl were raped repeatedly. But even in the moments when she suffered the greatest shame, Jackie prayed for her captors and spoke to them about God's love. Her face did not show panic, revulsion, or hatred, but glowed with the brightness of God's light.

During her imprisonment, she led the team in singing God's praises and presented the Gospel to her captors. One of the rioting inmates threw down his gun and received Jesus as his Saviour.

On the third day, there was a shoot-out between the prisoners and soldiers who came to stop the riot. Jackie and Juliet, a 16-year-old, were shot. Even as Jackie lay dying, she raised her hands to God, praying for the rioting inmates and for the soldiers. She died while singing to God.

Jackie had seen a vision of her impending martyrdom which she had shared with friends. She knew what could happen. So why did she expose herself and others to such danger? She went to the extreme in her love for Christ.

God Himself did the most extreme thing by sending His Son to die for us. Two thousand years ago, Israel was not a good place to send the Messiah. It would have been wiser to wait and send Him to a modern, democratic country where He would not have been crucified. Yet God gave His Son to endure the worst in order to bring the worst to the best place in eternity.

Those like Jackie give their lives with joy to share this love.

Very rarely will anyone die for a righteous man, though for a good man someone might possibly dare to die.

But God demonstrates his own love for us in this: While we were still sinners, Christ died for us.

Paul the Apostle
Martyred in Rome, AD 65
(ROMANS 5:7,8 NIV)

"It Is Not Difficult to Be a Christian"

Petrus Kristian
Indonesia
1996

"My name is Petrus Kristian. I am the oldest son of Pastor Ishak Kristian, who was burned to death a few months ago. It happened on October 10, 1996. At 11:30 A.M., about twenty people came and surrounded the church. My father, the pastor, tried calming those angry people, but they did not move away from the church. My father went into the house and prayed with six other people, including the rest of my family.

"Thirty minutes later, about 200 people came on foot bringing many kinds of tools. They started smashing the church building and parsonage. Six of the people in the house, including my father, ran and hid in a room at the back of the house. The other person hid upstairs where he was safe. Some of those angry people saw them and told them to get out of the room. Since they did not leave, the people started burning the building.

"One of those seven people, Didit (a church worker) ran through the fire and escaped. My father, mother, sister, cousin, and a church worker were trapped in the house and burned to death.

"During the fire, the local police did not take any action, probably because they were afraid of the mob. I hurried to the church at 1:30 P.M. but by that time, all were gone. The army, whose military base was four kilometres from town, were at military training elsewhere and were not available.

When they arrived at 5:00 P.M. to guard the area, everything was in ashes.

"The night before the funeral, a local government official apologized. He advised me not to take revenge. He also said that the incident might be my family's fate. (This is Muslim teaching — the will of Allah.)

"At first, I was really disappointed because I lost all of my beloved people. But this made me realize that material things around me are not eternal or worth loving. After the fire, most of our congregation became stronger in faith.

"Because we have Jesus, it is not difficult to be a Christian, although there are many oppressions."

Whatever we do, it is because Christ's love controls us.... Those who receive his new life will no longer live to please themselves. Instead, they will live to please Christ, who died and was raised for them.

Paul the Apostle
Martyred in Rome, AD 65
(2 CORINTHIANS 5:14,15 NLT)

Since Jesus went through everything you're going through and more, learn to think like him. Think of your sufferings as a weaning from that old sinful habit of always expecting to get your own way. Then you'll be able to live out your days free to pursue what God wants instead of being tyrannized by what you want.

Peter the Apostle
Crucified upside-down in Rome, AD 65
(1 PETER 4:1,2 THE MESSAGE)

Sin loses its power over us when we lay our lives down for Christ — because our eyes are on Jesus.

dc Talk

Sealed With His Blood

John Huss
Czechoslovakia
1415

"John Huss!"

The prisoner stood as the guard called his name. He blinked as he stepped from the prison darkness into the daylight. As soon as he saw the four bishops, he knew what was going on. They had come to find out if he would continue his stand — or if he would back down.

With the bishops was his friend, Lord John de Clum, who ran towards him. "Master John Huss, I encourage you: If you know you are guilty of any of the charges brought against you, don't be ashamed to admit you were wrong and change your mind."

John de Clum paused, searching for the words that would strengthen his friend. "On the other hand, please don't betray your own conscience. It is better to suffer any punishment, than deny what you have known to be the truth."

With tears in his eyes, John Huss faced his friend. "As the Most High God is my witness, I am ready with my heart and mind to change my stand if the Council can teach me by the holy Scripture and convict me of error."

The bishops murmured among themselves, "See how stubborn he is."

"He is so full of pride, he prefers his own thinking over the opinions of the whole Council."

"He will not change, but will continue in his errors."

Seeing that even the threat of death was not enough to change Huss' mind, they commanded the keepers to return him to his cell. The next day he would be sentenced to death.

John Huss was a priest in what is now Czechoslovakia. He was one of the first Christians to raise his voice for religious freedom and the right for an individual to have a personal relationship with God. He boldly confronted powerful church leaders who were not living Christlike lives. He also stood against the death sentence for those who didn't agree with the teaching of the church.

Huss had been expelled from the church for his beliefs several years earlier. Nevertheless, he continued to preach with great boldness, winning the admiration of the common people and the nobles. In 1413, he was summoned to appear before the church council in Constance. He went willingly; he welcomed the chance to explain his beliefs and the truths he had discovered before the leaders of the faith. But it was a trap.

Huss was never allowed to present his beliefs, but instead was thrown in prison. After nineteen months, he was finally put on trial. Every time John opened his mouth to defend himself, the crowd of people made so much noise he couldn't be heard. Finally, they simply read the charges against him and then read portions of his books as his answers.

They told him, "If you will humbly confess that you have been wrong, promise never to teach these things again, and publicly take back all you have said, we will have mercy on you and restore your honour."

"I am in the sight of the Lord my God," John replied with tears. "I can by no means do what you want me to do. How could I face God? How could I face the great number of people I have taught? They now have the most firm and certain knowledge of the Scriptures and are armed against all the assaults of Satan. How can I, by my example, make them uncertain? I cannot value my own body more than their health and salvation!"

They dressed him in priestly robes and ornaments — and then took turns removing the things they had just put on him. They did this to show they were stripping away his privileges as a priest. Finally, the only thing remaining that made him look like a priest was his hair: it was shaved bald on top. In the end, they removed this too, cutting off the skin on the top of his head with a pair of scissors. Finally he was condemned to death by fire.

John Huss was led outside the gates, with the whole city following after him. When he reached the place of execution, he knelt and prayed Psalm 31 and Psalm 51, and then said cheerfully, "Into Thy hands, O Lord, I commit my spirit: thou has redeemed me, O most good and merciful God!"

Pulling him up from his prayers, the hangman tied him to the stake with wet ropes. His neck was tied to the stake with a chain. Seeing it, John smiled and told his executioners, "My Lord Jesus Christ was bound with a harder chain than this for my sake, and why then should I be ashamed of this rusty one?"

Bundles of sticks were placed around him, reaching up to his chin.

Given one last chance to renounce his errors, John replied, "What error should I renounce? I am guilty of no wrong. I taught all men repentance and remission of sins, according to the truth of the Gospel of Jesus Christ. For that Gospel I am here, with a cheerful mind and courage, ready to suffer death. *What I taught with my lips I now seal with my blood.*"

As the fire was lit, John Huss began to sing a hymn with such a loud and cheerful voice that he was heard over the crackling of the fire and the jeers of the crowd. His song: "Jesus Christ! the Son of the living God! Have mercy on me."

John Huss chose to die rather than to deny the truths he had learned from the Scriptures. He trusted in the Lord to comfort and strengthen him, and Jesus did. History records that during his trial, his friend John de Clum comforted him greatly: "No tongue can express what courage he received by the short talk which he had with him, when in so great a broil and grievous hatred, he saw himself forsaken of all men."

"I Am God"

Reck
Romania
1950s

Suddenly the Communist stopped beating the Christian prisoner. After a short pause, he said: "You know, I am God. I have power of life and death over you. The one who is in heaven cannot decide to keep you in life. Everything depends upon me. If I wish, you live. If I wish, you are killed. *I am God!*"

In the midst of his suffering, Reck replied, "You don't know what a deep thing you have said. Every caterpillar is in reality a butterfly, *if it develops right*. You have not been created to be a torturer, a man who kills. You have been created to become like God, with the life of the Godhead in your heart.

"Many who have been persecutors like you have come to realize — like the apostle Paul — that it is shameful for a man to commit atrocities, that they can do much better things. So they have become partakers of the divine nature.

"Jesus said to the Jews of His time, 'Ye are gods.' Believe me, your real calling is to be Godlike — to have the character of God, not a torturer."

At that moment, the Communist did not pay much attention to the words of his victim. But those words worked in his heart, and he remembered them long afterwards. Eventually, he became a Christian.

"If You Tell Others, People Will Kill You"

Masih
(This name has been changed to protect the individual)
Pakistan
1990s

Masih was an active Islamic student and argued with Christian students. He couldn't understand their opinions. Eventually they humbly offered to help Masih learn more about Jesus. He had many questions about Him which they answered.

But Masih was not satisfied. He went to some Muslim clerics who were his friends. They said, "Christians told you this. Don't be deceived by them." Masih felt they were avoiding his questions and pressed them for specific answers. In the end, they gave the same answers that the Christians did.

Still, Masih needed more proof. He eventually went to another priest who was a friend and asked him the same questions about Jesus. The priest told him, "What Christians told you is true, but if you tell others, people will kill you."

When Masih heard this, he went to a Christian pastor. The pastor told him about Jesus as Saviour by using both the Koran and the Bible. As he compared the texts, Masih slowly came to the realization that the Koran did not tell the whole story about Jesus. In his own heart he realized that Jesus was the truth and any sincere student of truth must follow the Jesus of the Bible, not of the Koran.

Masih told us in his own words what happened after he came to this realization:

"My family kicked me out. My brother returned from Germany and threatened to kill me; but if God is for me, who can be against me?

"My parents said I was kidnapped by Christians. They accused the Christian pastor. I gave court testimony for the pastor, clearing him. I then hid with Christians in another city and went to theological seminary.

"My brother from Jordan did not threaten me, but invited me to visit and told me: 'Don't tell Jordanians you are a Christian.' When he heard I had become a pastor, he and his family didn't want to see me.

"I am now an ordained pastor and was married two months ago. I am happy in Jesus. Although I lost my physical family, I have my spiritual family.

"Now I help my Christian brothers and sisters to understand Muslims and lead them to Christ."

"We've given up everything to follow you," [Peter] said.

And Jesus replied, "I assure you that everyone who has given up house or brothers or sisters or mother or father or children or property, for my sake and for the Good News, will receive now in return, a hundred times over, houses, brothers, sisters, mothers, children, and property — with persecutions. And in the world to come they will have eternal life."

Jesus
(MARK 10:28-31 NLT)

"What Harm Can a Little Girl Do?"

Linh Dao
Vietnam
1991

Four police officers suddenly burst into ten-year-old Linh Dao's home. They forced her father, an underground pastor in North Vietnam, to remain seated while the authorities ransacked the home searching for Bibles.

"I remember when the police came," Linh Dao recalls. "They searched around the house all of that morning and asked many different questions. It was scary to talk to the policemen, but I knew what they were looking for, so I concentrated and tried my best not to be scared or nervous." As the police questioned her parents, Linh courageously hid some of the Bibles in her school knapsack.

When the police asked her about the contents of the knapsack, Linh simply replied, "It is books for children."

Linh Dao's father was arrested that day and sentenced to seven years of re-education through hard labour.

"When the policemen decided to take my dad away, all of my family knelt down and prayed. I prayed first, then my sister, then my mum, and last of all, my dad. I prayed that my dad would have peace and remain healthy and that my family would survive these hard times. We were all crying, but I told myself I have to face what's happening now."

Word quickly spread about the arrest, and neighbouring children began to ask Linh what criminal acts her father had done. She told her friends, "My father is not a criminal. He is a Christian, and I am proud of him for not wavering in his faith!"

As each day passed, Linh Dao made a mark on her wooden bookcase as she prayed for her father. She remembers, "I cried almost every single night because I worried how my father was doing in prison and how the policemen were treating him.

"Before my dad was in prison, I was just a child. I didn't need to worry about anything. It was a lot different after my dad left. My mind got older very quickly. I told my sister that we had to help Mum do the work around the house, so she could continue to do my dad's work in the church.

"I prayed every day and every night. My faith grew very fast. I knew one thing that I had to concentrate on and that was spending time learning from the Bible so when I grew up, I could be like my dad, sharing and preaching. When I think about this, I feel my heart burning inside me, pushing me, telling me this is the right thing to do."

Finally, after more than a year, Linh, her mother, and sister were able to visit their father in prison. When they reached the compound, they were separated by a chain fence. Linh quickly discovered that she could squeeze into the prison yard through a chained gate. She ran to her father and hugged him tightly. The guards watched the little girl but, surprisingly, left her alone. *What harm can a little girl do?* they must have thought.

Little did they know! Armed with innocence and child-like faith, children are a secret weapon against the kingdom of Satan. During that first visit to her father's prison, Linh was able to smuggle him a pen, which he used to write scriptures and sermons on cigarette paper. These "cigarette sermons" travelled from cell to cell and were instrumental in bringing many prisoners to Christ.

Linh Dao's prayers were answered. Her father was released early, before he had served all seven years of his sentence. "It was a big surprise when I came home from school one day and saw my dad had been released from prison. I ran and then gave him a big hug. We were so happy. I was proud of my family and I wanted to yell and let the whole world know that I wasn't scared of anything because God always protects each step I go in my life."

Linh Dao is now a teenager. She desires to follow in the footsteps of her father and be a preacher of the Gospel of Jesus Christ. She knows firsthand the dangers of sharing her faith in Communist Vietnam and remains determined to obey Christ rather than men. In spite of a "grim future," she spends her time in intense Bible study.

Don't underestimate what you, as one person, can do. God will work through anyone who is submitted to Him — of any age — to accomplish His will on the earth.

Just look at what Moses discovered: If one man or woman is willing to obey God, it can change the destiny of millions.

Ambassador for Christ

Boris (pseudonym)
U.S.S.R.
1970s

Finally the inmates' mocking laughter stopped.

Boris did not smile.

On purpose — to humiliate him for his faith in Christ — the prison guards had issued him a uniform that was twice his size. The sleeves reached his knees; his gigantic shoes made him look like a clown. When he entered the barracks, the criminals, incited by the camp commander, greeted him with laughter and ridicule.

A prisoner came and bowed in front of him with fake piety. "I greet you, Holy Father. You are the Ambassador of Christ Himself. Do you represent the interests of heaven?"

His mocking words gave Boris courage. He forgot how ridiculous he looked and boldly answered, "Yes, I do represent heaven. That is why the atheists hate me and have imprisoned me."

Boris recalled, "While I was preaching to those despising sinners, the sermon affected me too. Soon, I wanted to hug them for having reminded me of my high calling!

Many fear suffering; in the past, I too feared. But the presence of the Lord in jail has given me so many happy

experiences that I would not have changed them for years of easy living in freedom.

Boris

We are Christ's ambassadors, and God is using us to speak to you. We urge you, as though Christ himself were here pleading with you, "Be reconciled to God!"

Paul the Apostle
Martyred in Rome, AD 65
(2 CORINTHIANS 5:20 NLT)

A Crown of Eternal Glory

Romanus
Antioch (now Antakya, Turkey)
circa AD 285

"Are you the author of this rebellion?" the Roman prefect raged. "Are you the reason so many were willing to lose their lives? By the gods, I swear you shall suffer for it. In your body you will suffer the pains you have encouraged your fellows to bear."

Romanus boldly answered, "Your sentence, O Prefect, I joyfully embrace. I am willing to be sacrificed for my brethren by as cruel means as you may invent."

The Roman prefect Asclepiades had invaded the city of Antioch, intending to force the Christians to renounce their faith. But Romanus had encouraged them to fight back. As soldiers were marching to break up a worship service, Romanus burst into the service saying, "The wolves are on the way to devour this flock, but fear not, my brethren!"

As the believers saw the great grace of God working in Romanus, old men and women, fathers and mothers, young men and maidens were greatly encouraged to stand firm, ready to shed their blood for the name of their Christ. With one will and mind, they were able to fight off the armed Roman soldiers.

Asclepiades had Romanus scourged with whips. But instead of tears, sighs, and groans, Romanus sang psalms all the time of his whipping. The more the martyr said about the Lord Jesus, the more furious the prefect became. He commanded the martyr's sides to be slit with knives until the bones showed white.

Romanus continued to preach the living God, the Lord Jesus Christ, His well-beloved Son, and eternal life through faith in His blood. This time, the prefect ordered that his teeth be knocked out, so he couldn't speak clearly. His face was beat, his beard pulled out, his cheeks were gashed with knives. When they were finished, Romanus said, "I thank thee, O Prefect. Look how many wounds I have, so many mouths I have whereby I may preach my Lord and Saviour Christ, and praise God."

The Roman prefect was astonished with Romanus' unwavering commitment to Christ. He commanded the tortures to cease. He threatened to burn him. He blasphemed God, saying, "Your crucified Christ is but a yesterday's God; the gods of the Gentiles are most ancient."

Romanus then preached on the eternity of Christ, His human nature, of His death for all mankind. Then he said, "Give me a child, O Prefect, one who is only seven years old, and not yet spoiled by malice and vice. You will hear what he has to say."

A little boy was called out of the crowd. "Tell me, child," said the martyr, "whether we should worship one Christ, and in Christ one Father, or should we worship many gods?"

"God is one and unique," the child answered. "We children cannot believe that there are many gods."

The prefect was amazed and said, "Where did you learn this lesson?"

"From my mother," answered the child. "With her milk I sucked in this lesson, that I must believe in Christ."

The mother was called, and she gladly appeared. The prefect commanded the child to be whipped. The crowd of people watching could not keep from crying. The mother alone stood dry-eyed, reminding her child of stories from the Scriptures of others who suffered. She called to her son, "Hold fast, my child. Soon you shall pass to Him who will give you a crown of eternal glory."

The mother smiled her encouragement. The child was encouraged and received the stripes with a smiling face.

The prefect commanded the child's head to be cut off. The mother kissed him, saying, "Farewell, my sweet child. When you have entered the kingdom of Christ, remember your mother."

As the sword came down on her child's neck, she sang:

"All laud and praise with heart and voice,

O Lord, we yield to thee:

To whom the death of this thy saint,

We know most dear to be."

Asclepiades returned to torturing Romanus. He was cast into a mighty fire, but a great storm arose and quenched the fire. Finally, the prefect, amazed at Romanus' courage, commanded him to be brought back into the prison and strangled.

When threatened with death, Jesus Freaks aren't afraid. This continually surprises those who don't believe in God, who think that when you are dead, your life is over.

You can kill us, but you cannot do us any real harm.

Justin Martyr
Martyred in Rome, AD 165

*My dear Jesus, my Saviour, is so deeply
written in my heart, that I feel confident,
that if my heart were to be cut open and
chopped to pieces, the name of Jesus would
be found written on every piece.*

Ignatius
A student under John
Devoured by wild animals in Rome
AD 111

"I Learned to See God"

Young Girl
Mainland China
During the Red Guard Era, 1966-1969

A Chinese girl refused to betray the secrets of the underground church, even though she had been tortured again and again. She was asked how she could bear so much suffering.

"It was not hard," she replied. "I had been taught by my pastor that the real torture lasts very little. For one minute of torture, there are ten minutes of glancing at the enraged faces and the implements of pain. I decided to keep my eyes closed the whole time. I did not see the stick before it hit me or afterwards. The suffering was much reduced.

"I relied on the promise of Jesus: 'Blessed are the pure in heart, for they shall see God.' I purified my heart of the fear of men, and I learned to see God. When the Communists became aware of my defence, they stuck my eyelids open with tape, but it was too late. My vision had already taken on a new aspect, and I had seen God as so many had seen Him before."

Nothing between us and God, our faces shining with the brightness of his face. And so we are transfigured much like the Messiah, our lives gradually becoming brighter and more beautiful as God enters our lives and we become like him.

Paul the Apostle
Martyred in Rome, AD 65
(2 CORINTHIANS 3:18 THE MESSAGE)

Hungry for God's Word

Joan Waste
Derby, England
1550s

The ragged old man looked up as the young woman entered his cell. He had to admire her faithfulness. Even though she was totally blind, Joan Waste made her way through the streets of Derby, rain or shine. "Hello, John Hurt," she called cheerfully. Holding out a small book, she asked, "Please, can you read to me today?"

"What chapter would you like to hear?" the old man answered, smiling. Locked in debtor's prison, with never a visitor besides Joan, he had little else to do.

Although Joan Waste was born blind, she was never idle. When she was little, she helped her father make rope. Later, when she was twelve, she learned to knit socks and sleeves. She kept practising and practising until she knitted very well.

During the reign of King Edward, churches began to offer readings from the Bible in English instead of only in Latin. Joan went to church daily to hear the Word of God, and it dramatically changed her life. She had a tremendous desire to understand Scripture and have it printed in her memory. Even though she was blind and could not read, and New Testaments were expensive, she decided to get one of her own. Since she was from a poor family, it took her a long time to save enough money to buy one.

Then Joan had to find someone who would read to her. That's when she met John Hurt, who agreed to read her a chapter a day. On days when he was too sick to read, she would pay others to read to her. Joan had an unusually good memory, and she became very familiar with the Bible. By the time she was twenty-two, she could repeat many entire chapters by heart.

When Queen Mary took the throne, laws were passed making it illegal to own a Bible in English. Joan was brought before the bishop because of her beliefs, charged with heresy, and put in prison. She was questioned again and again. Finally, she said, "I cannot forsake the truth. I beg you, please stop troubling me." After that, she wouldn't say anything else.

The death sentence was finally pronounced and she was handed over to the sheriff. On August 1, 1556, she was led to the stake. There, she knelt down and prayed. Then she stood up. "Please pray for me," she urged everyone watching. The executioner fastened her to the stake and the flames were lit.

Joan treasured the Word of God, going to great trouble to store it in her heart. The truths she found in its pages brought her great strength.

Many people today have access to Scripture, but never take the time to memorize it and meditate on it. Do you?

I bless God for my imprisonment, for I then began to relish the life and sweetness of God's Holy Word.

Nicholas Caren
Martyred in England
1539

Finish the Race

Saul of Tarsus
Roman Empire
AD 35

"Ananias!"

The voice was clear. "Yes, Lord," Ananias answered.

"Go over to Straight Street, to the house of Judas. When you arrive, ask for a man from Tarsus. His name is Saul. He has just had a vision in which he saw a man named Ananias come in and lay hands on him so he could see again."

"But Lord," Ananias exclaimed, "everybody's been talking about this man and the terrible things he's done to the believers in Jerusalem. And now he's shown up here in Damascus with papers from the chief priest, authorizing him to arrest every believer in town!"

But Jesus said, "Go! I've picked Saul as my personal representative to take My message to the Gentiles, to kings, and to the people of Israel. I'm about to show him what he must suffer for My name."

Ananias obeyed Jesus and found Saul. He laid his hands on him and said, "Brother Saul, the Lord Jesus, whom you saw on your way here, sent me so you could see again and be filled with the Holy Spirit." Instantly, something like scales fell from Saul's eyes, and he could see again. He got up, was baptized, and then sat down and ate a hearty meal.

Saul stayed with the believers in Damascus for a few days. Then he went right to work, preaching in the meeting places, saying "Jesus really is the Son of God!"

Everyone who heard him was amazed. "Isn't this the same man who persecuted Jesus' followers so badly in Jerusalem? Didn't he come here to drag even more Christians off to jail?"

Every day, Saul's preaching got more powerful. Soon the Jews in Damascus couldn't argue with him or refute his proofs that Jesus was the Messiah. After a while, they decided to kill Saul, but he found out about their plot. He escaped from the city by being lowered over the city wall in a large basket.

Back in Jerusalem, Saul tried to join the disciples, but they didn't trust him yet. Then Barnabas, a trusted friend of theirs spoke on his behalf, "The Lord dramatically revealed Himself to Saul on the road to Damascus. Since then, Saul has laid his life on the line, boldly preaching in the synagogues in Jesus' name." After that, the disciples accepted Saul as one of them.

Saul preached boldly in the name of the Lord all over Jerusalem. When the Jews there attempted to kill him, the other believers got him safely out of town, took him to Caesarea, and then sent him on to his hometown of Tarsus.

It was God's plan for Paul to write the Bible, not to die as a zealous new convert!

In the years that followed, Saul, who had changed his name to Paul, escaped death repeatedly. An angry mob in Iconium tried to stone him along with his friend Barnabas, but they were able to escape to Lystra. Another time, the Jews from Iconium who were chasing Paul and Barnabas were able to turn a murderous mob against them. They stoned Paul and dragged him out of the city, leaving him for dead. But when the disciples gathered around him, Paul was miraculously able to stand and walk back into the city. The next morning Paul and Barnabas left for Derbe.

Time and again, Paul was caught, and time and again, he escaped. He was thrown in prison at Philippi, but in the night God sent an earthquake. The prison doors were opened and Paul's chains fell off. Later, he was imprisoned in Jerusalem until forty men swore to neither eat nor drink until they saw Paul dead. When the Romans found out, they moved him to Caesarea. He was in jail there for two years, and then sent to Rome to be tried before Caesar. On the way, he survived shipwreck only to be bitten by a deadly, poisonous snake. Paul shook the snake off into the fire, preached the Gospel, and many were saved.

In a letter to the church at Corinth, Paul gives a brief account of all of his sufferings: "I have worked harder, been put in jail more often, been whipped times without number, and faced death again and again. Five different times the Jews gave me thirty-nine lashes. Three times I was beaten with rods. Once I was stoned. Three times I was shipwrecked. Once I spent a whole night and a day adrift at sea.

"I have travelled many weary miles. I have faced danger from flooded rivers and from robbers. I have faced danger from my own people, the Jews, as well as from the Gentiles. I have faced danger in the cities, in the deserts, and on the stormy seas. And I have faced danger from men who claim to be Christians and are not. I have lived with weariness and pain and sleepless nights. Often I have been hungry and thirsty and have gone without food. Often I have shivered with cold, without enough clothing to keep me warm" (2 Corinthians 11:23-27 NLT).

Paul survived all this and finally reached Rome around AD 55. There, he was put under house arrest until his trial before Caesar. Most ancient writers agree that, although nearly all his friends left him, he defended himself before Caesar so cleverly that he was set free for a time. After more missionary journeys, he was again arrested, and by this time being a follower of Jesus carried the death penalty.

As Paul's execution drew near, God prepared his heart. He wrote to his spiritual son Timothy, "Now the time has come for me to die. My life is like a drink offering being poured out on the altar. I have fought well, I have finished the race, and I have been faithful. So a crown will be given to me for pleasing the Lord" (2 Timothy 4:6-8 CEV).

Finally, Paul was sentenced to death. Because he was a Roman citizen, he was not tortured like so many of the believers were during Nero's reign, but was beheaded outside the city. He was approximately 64 years old.

There is a time to resist persecution and escape. We have seen how Paul did. Jesus did also. He walked through the middle of a crowd in Nazareth who wanted to throw him off a cliff (Luke 4:28-30). He walked through the midst of a crowd in Jerusalem who tried to stone Him (John 8:59). Later, other Jewish leaders tried to arrest Him, but He escaped out of their hands (John 10:39). On the night He was betrayed, when He said, "I am He," the soldiers drew back and fell to the ground (John 18:6). Jesus could have escaped, but this time, He didn't.

Jesus Freaks know God well enough to know His will for their lives and when that will is accomplished. Paul knew he had finished his race and it was all right for him to go home to be with the Lord. Until he knew that, he always kept his eyes of faith looking for God's grace to either deliver him, help him endure, and even raise him from the dead. He refused to quit until he'd won!

For to me, living is for Christ, and dying is even better. Yet if I live, that means fruitful service for Christ. I really don't know which is better. I'm torn between two desires: Sometimes I want to live, and sometimes I long to go and be with Christ. That would be far better for me, but it is better for you that I live. I am convinced of this, so I will continue with you so that you will grow and experience the joy of your faith.

Paul the Apostle
Written while in prison awaiting execution; he was released some time later
(PHILIPPIANS 1:21-25 NLT)

Even the best of Christians are troubled by the question, "Why does an almighty God send, or at least allow, suffering?" When you are nagged by thoughts like this, say to yourself, "I am still in elementary school. When I graduate from the university of Christian life, I will understand His ways better and doubts will cease."

Richard Wurmbrand
Imprisoned for a total of 14 years
Romania
1940s, 50s, and 60s

"If You Love Jesus, Don't Sing"

Tom White
Cuba
1979–1980

"Well, this isn't bad," Tom White mumbled to himself. He stood in a pitch-black, cold room. He could feel the wind pouring into the room from a vent above the door. Exploring the cell, he found a bed with broken springs, a stinking mattress, and an old wooden chair nailed to the floor.

He lay down, but sleep was impossible. It was just too cold. His sleeveless coveralls were made of thin cotton, so they weren't much help. He wondered how long he could stay alive in this room.

Tom White, an American Christian, had made many successful drops of Gospel literature over Cuba, distributing more than 400,000 pieces. But on May 27, 1979, his small plane crash-landed on a Cuban highway, just as he had finished a night drop. He was immediately arrested by the Communists, who questioned him and put him in solitary confinement.

Finally the guards put a hood over his head and took him to a little room for more questioning. "It sure is warm today, isn't it?" the captain taunted, taking off his military jacket to begin the interrogation. "Who do you work for?"

"I work for Jesus."

"Oh, is that right? And how much money did this Jesus pay you for making these trips?"

"I took these trips for no pay. My pay is the love and blessing that God gives me for obeying Him."

Most of the captain's questions centred around money, the CIA, and revolution. These were the only concepts of power that he seemed to understand. After three or four days of cold and little sleep, White was too tired to even follow his train of thought. He sat in front of his interrogator, his head dropping, his thoughts wandering.

"How can I fight this? This could go on forever," White asked himself. Suddenly he had his answer. He explains:

"The Holy Spirit gave me a measure of pity and compassion for this man who was more in prison than I. I stopped responding to his questions and stared directly into his eyes. 'Oh, God, help Captain Santos,' I prayed. 'Break through, Jesus. He is the one in the cold, for he has never felt the warmth of Your love.' I continued to pray in front of him like this for hours. His questions came less frequently until he finally stopped."

"What are you doing?" he demanded.

"I'm praying for you."

The captain's mouth dropped open. He ran one hand back through his hair, then rummaged for a cigarette. This was the first time White had seen him smoke. The prisoner continued to sit rigidly as he was required, looking at Santos and praying.

The captain looked nervously around the room, then started drumming his fingers on the desk. In the next session White was surprised to see him wearing sunglasses. Evidently he didn't want White to see his eyes. *That's all right. God doesn't need eye contact. He deals with the heart,* White thought, and continued praying.

Santos sent for Major Alvarez. The major was always his last resort. Alvarez stormed into the room, red-faced and angry as usual. "So, you think this is a game?" he screamed, pounding on the desk for emphasis. "Now we are going to send you to see the third foot of the cat."

White remembers, "I was thrown into another room. Following the wall in the blackness, I discovered there was no bed or chair. The blower vent over the door was fully open. The air was pouring out at such a terrific rate that my hair was blown straight out from my head.

"I tried to walk in the pitch blackness to keep warm, holding my hands out to keep from bumping into the wall. But the wall was too cold to touch. Besides, rather than warming me, walking only brought me close to the vent. I huddled in the corner of the room.

"'Oh God, help me!' I cried out in despair. He would, only not in the way I wanted. I stuffed my coverall legs into my socks to keep the air from coming up my trousers, then pulled my arms inside the sleeveless top. I stretched the top up over my nose so I could heat my body with my warm breath. This gave me times of relief, but then fatigue and slow but steady loss of body heat would cause me to start shaking. I couldn't bear to sit on the floor, nor lean on the wall. The only position that worked was standing with just my forehead touching the wall.

"I don't know why I remembered to sing. But God's hand was guiding and teaching me. As the levels of punishment grew more severe, so did the intensity of spiritual warfare.

Satan tried harder to drag me down, but God gently raised me up. Psalm 3:3 says, He is my glory and the lifter up of mine head. God was gracious, merciful, and loving, asking only for a chance to prove Himself to me.

"I started singing that great hymn, 'A Mighty Fortress Is Our God.' I sang 'Jesus Loves Me,' Bible choruses, and every Christian song I could remember. I was no longer conscious of the cold, only of Jesus. With eyes closed, my head barely touching the wall, I whistled, sang, even imitated a trumpet blasting out praises to the Lord.

"Although I didn't think through the many Scriptures which support it, I had entered the highest level of warfare against the enemy — praise. Psalm 22:3 says that God inhabits our praises. I don't know how this is accomplished, but it's true. The mighty Deliverer, the Messiah, the Saviour was with me. He held my shaking body in His arms. I was with Jesus, no matter what happened."

A guard opened the little steel window flap in the door and peered inside curiously.

"What are you doing?" he demanded.

"I'm singing about Jesus."

"Why?"

"Because I love Him," White replied happily.

He slammed the flap and left. White continued singing.

He returned a few minutes later and opened the window flap again. "If you love Jesus, don't sing," he ordered, then left. But White loved Jesus too much to stop singing.

Over the next two days the guards came to check on him every three or four hours. The flap would open and a flashlight beam would snake across the floor looking for him. Still White continued to sing. At the end of those two days, he was returned to his former cell which, though still cold, seemed warm in comparison. Now convinced that he was not a super-spy trying to overthrow their government, they had started White back up the treatment ladder.

After three months, Tom White was moved from solitary confinement to the main prison where 7,000 prisoners were kept. There he met and worshipped with members of the Cuban church who were imprisoned for their faith.

An international campaign for his release helped reduce White's prison time from his original 24-year sentence. After many prayers, letters, appeals from U.S. Congressmen and even Mother Teresa, he was released on October 27, 1980, after seventeen months in jail. He now serves as U.S. director for The Voice of the Martyrs.

"Let Christ Help You"

Zenobius and Zenobia
Aegaea, Cilicia
(near Kalamaki-Aydin, Turkey)
AD 285

"I love Jesus Christ more than all the riches and honour of this world. Death and the torments with which you threaten me, I do not consider a disadvantage, but my greatest gain." Having said that, Zenobius, the Bishop of the Church of Aegaea, looked steadily at Lysias, the Roman proconsul.

Lysias had offered Zenobius great wealth, honour, and position if he would follow the command of the Emperor and serve the Roman gods, but threatened him with torture if he did not.

On a tour through the provinces of Cilicia, Lysias had been holding criminal court against Christians in town after town. He had been in Aegaea only a short time, but had already tortured five Christians to death. Now he looked forward to tormenting the bishop himself.

"Put him on the rack!" the proconsul ordered. "We will see how much pain he can stand."

While the executioners were busy with Zenobius, his sister Zenobia, having heard what was happening, came running in. She cried with a loud voice, "You tyrant! What evil thing has my brother done, that you torture him like this?" She too was seized by the servants, stripped naked, stretched out, and roasted beside her brother on a red-hot iron bed.

The tyrant mocking the martyrs said, "Now let Christ come and help you, seeing you suffer these torments for Him."

Zenobius replied: "See, He is already with us, and cools, with His heavenly dew, the flames of fire on our bodies; though you, surrounded as you are with the thick darkness of wickedness, cannot see it."

That made Lysias furious. "Throw them into boiling pots of water!" he hollered. Miraculously, the boiling water did not kill the two believers, and they continued to praise the Lord Jesus. Lysias was almost beside himself. None of the other Christians had survived his torments like these two had. "Get them out of my sight!"

"What shall we do to them next?" the executioners asked.

At his wits' end, Lysias ordered a form of death that was sure to work but seldom used on Christians because it was quick and painless: "Take them out of the city and behead them." Their bodies were buried in a cave near the place where they were executed.

Like other martyrs before and after them, Zenobius and Zenobia experienced the reality of God's presence.

The Father is a merciful God, who always gives us comfort... We share in the terrible sufferings of Christ, but also in the wonderful comfort he gives.

Paul the Apostle
Martyred in Rome, AD 65
(2 CORINTHIANS 1:3,5 CEV)

A Burnt Offering

Philip
Sudan
1996

The guards picked up a burning log from the fire.

"Renounce your faith in Jesus Christ!" they commanded. "We will burn you and cut you until you become a Muslim." Philip had been taken to a military barracks along with thirty-five other Christians. Islamic officials began to beat them and curse them.

For eleven days, Philip and several of his friends were bound, beaten, and burned as government soldiers tried to convert them to the Islamic faith. None of the twelve women survived the torture. Philip still bears the scars on his chest left by the burning log used to torture him. He later told reporters:

"My faith was very strong when they burned me. I prayed, 'God I will never forget You.' I refused to be a Muslim because I knew God was with me."

The Bible tells us everyone who wants to live a godly life in Christ Jesus will be persecuted (2 Timothy 3:12). Philip has paid a heavy price for his faith in Jesus. His body became as a burnt offering to the Lord. But he did not turn away from Jesus and Jesus did not turn away from him. God stayed with him and gave him the grace to withstand the torture.

A Mighty Fortress Is Our God

And though this world, with devils filled,
should threaten to undo us;
We will not fear, for God hath willed
His truth to triumph through us;
    The prince of darkness grim,
we tremble not for him;
His rage we can endure,
For lo! his doom is sure,
One little word shall fell him.
That word above all earthly powers,
No thanks to them, abideth,
The Spirit and the gifts are ours
Through Him who with us sideth;
    Let goods and kindred go,
This mortal life also;
The body they may kill;
God's truth abideth still,
His kingdom is forever.

Verses 3 and 4
Hymn by Martin Luther
Father of the Reformation
Tried for heresy, 1521
1483-1546

Praising God, whether in psalms, in hymns, or in spir-
itual songs, gives tremendous strength to the believer.

This hymn, written by a Jesus Freak in the 1500s, has helped Christians for centuries.

Martin Luther, the father of the Reformation, learned from the Bible that God saves men by His grace and that man cannot save himself through his own effort. After receiving this revelation, he developed his own theology, based completely on the Bible. This greatly angered the established church of that time, who called for his execution, but Luther evaded them.

At his trial, corrupt church leaders tried to get him to recant, but he refused, saying:

Unless I am convinced by Scripture and plain reason — I do not accept the authority of the popes and councils, for they have contradicted each other — my conscience is captive to the Word of God. I cannot and I will not recant anything for to go against conscience is neither right nor safe. God help me. Amen.

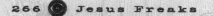

Two Chinese Christians were led
to torture and death.

One quoted Jesus' words,
"It is finished," in a whisper.

His brother answered, "No, that's not
what Jesus said when He suffered. He
said, 'It is accomplished.'"

"He Is Lord"

Pastor Selchun
Northern Nigeria
1992

Muslims in Kaduna, Nigeria, went on a rampage against Christians. Two pastors and their families were killed, along with 300 laymen. The fanatics severed Pastor Selchun's right hand. When it fell to the ground, he raised the other one and sang:

> "He is Lord, He is Lord!
> He is risen from the dead, and He is Lord.
> Every knee shall bow and every tongue confess
> that Jesus Christ is Lord."

His wife and sister stood by praying.

Islam is seeking to gain full control of Nigeria. Christians in the northern states have been the victims of rioting and looting. Churches have been destroyed and many Christians killed.

Pray for God's protection over brothers and sisters in such circumstances and that God will lead them as they face their persecutors. Also pray that God will take away the spiritual blindness of the persecutors as He did for Paul in Acts, chapter 9, and the Muslim priest Zahid, whose story is found earlier in this book.

"I Can't Bear Your Beatings!"

Pastor Florescu
Romania
1960s

The Communist torturers came towards Pastor Florescu again, this time with red-hot iron pokers. "Who else believes as you do? Give us their names." Florescu would not speak. They had already cut him again and again with knives and beaten him very badly. When he refused to cooperate, he was returned to his cell.

Starving rats were then driven into his cell through a large pipe. He could not sleep, having to defend himself at all times. If he rested a moment, the rats would attack him. He was forced to stand for two weeks, day and night. The Communists kept asking him to betray his brethren, but he resisted steadfastly.

In the end, they brought his fourteen-year-old son and began to whip the boy in front of his father, saying that they would continue to beat him until the pastor told them what they wanted to know. The poor man was half crazy. He bore it as long as he could. But when he could stand it no more, he cried to his son, "Alexander, I must say what they want! I can't bear your beatings anymore!"

The son answered, "Father, don't do me the injustice of having a traitor as a parent. Withstand! If they kill me, I will die with the words, 'Jesus and my fatherland.'"

This enraged the Communists. They grabbed the young man and beat him to death, his blood splattering over the walls of the cell. He died praising God.

People who live this way make it plain that they are looking for their true home...They were after a far better country...heaven country. You can see why God is so proud of them, and has a City waiting for them.

Hebrews 11:14,16
THE MESSAGE

I tell you this so you won't be ashamed by my death. If you love me, you will rejoice that God has called me to this honour, which is greater than any earthly honour I could ever attain. Who wouldn't be happy to die for this cause? I trust in my Lord God, who put His mind, will, and affection in my heart, and choose to lose all my worldly substance, and my life, too, rather than deny His known truth. He will comfort me, aid me, and strengthen me forever, even to the yielding of my spirit and soul into His hands.

Bishop Nicholas Ridley
Burned at the stake
Oxford, England
1555

Temporary, Light Affliction

John Jue Han Ding
Mainland China
During the Red Guard Era, 1966-69

John Jue Han Ding could feel the mighty power of God within him, strengthening him to endure the unbearable. They had tied his hands behind his back and then emptied a bucket of human waste on his head. They had left him like that for days, never giving him a chance to clean himself. He was given food, but with his hands tied behind his back, he had to lie on the floor and lick it up like an animal. The food had to pass through soiled lips. He still did not deny his faith and refused to admit to crimes he had not committed.

Then his torturers filled a cell with human waste and put him in it with a multitude of common criminals. Now they all waded and suffocated in it. The common criminals were told they would all be kept like this indefinitely unless they forced him to comply with the demands of the interrogators. To survive, these criminals now competed in torturing him day and night.

When he came to this point in his story, John stopped. His face started to glow, and he began to sing with a beautiful voice.

Here are the words of his song:

For our light affliction, which is but for a moment, is working for us a far more exceeding and eternal weight of glory, while we do not look at the things which are seen, but at the things which are not seen. For the things which

are seen are temporary, but the things which are not seen
are eternal.

2 CORINTHIANS 4:17,18 NKJV

The authorities eventually gave up and stopped trying to make John deny his faith. They then released him.

For God has said,
   "I will never fail you.
   I will never forsake you."

That is why we can say with confidence,
   "The Lord is my helper,
   so I will not be afraid.
   What can mere mortals do to me?"

Hebrews 13:5,6 NLT

The Last Scottish Martyr

Walter Milne
82 years old
Scotland
1551

Finally Oliphant, the archbishop's priest, faced the feeble old man. "Will you recant? If not, I will sentence you."

Walter Milne replied, "I am accused of my life. I know I must die once and therefore, as Christ said to Judas, what thou doest, do quickly. I will not recant the truth. I am corn, not chaff; I will not be blown away with the wind or burst by the flail. I will survive both."

Walter Milne, once a parish priest, heard the Gospel and was converted. He was put in prison for his beliefs, but he escaped. He hid for a while and then began to preach again. He was forced into hiding a second time, but was finally captured and tried for heresy at the age of eighty-two.

At his trial he was so feeble — both because of his age and the mistreatment he suffered in prison — that he couldn't climb the platform. Nevertheless, when he began to speak, he made the courtroom ring with such courage and power that the Christians who were present rejoiced.

One by one his beliefs were examined, and he did not give in. Oliphant sentenced Milne to be burned as a heretic, but his boldness and faith had so moved the heart of the mayor that he refused to be his judge. In fact, the whole town was so offended with Milne's unfair sentence that they refused to sell the bishop a single rope or tar barrel.

After much delay, everything was ready. When Oliphant ordered him to climb up to the stake, he refused. "No! By the law of God, I am forbidden to kill myself. But if you will put me up there and take part in my death, I will go up gladly."

Oliphant lifted the old man up to the stake. Milne prayed, then addressed the people:

"Dear friends, I do not suffer today for any crime, but only for the defence of the faith of Jesus Christ, as set forth in the Old and New Testament. As other faithful martyrs have offered themselves gladly, knowing that they will receive eternal joy, I praise God today, that He has called me also, to seal up His truth with my life.

"I have received this life from Him, and I willingly offer it for His glory. If you too would escape eternal death, depend only on Jesus Christ and His mercy, that you may be delivered from eternal judgment."

While Milne spoke, there was great mourning in the crowd. As the fire was lit, he cried, "Lord, have mercy on me! Pray, people, while there is time!"

The crowd was greatly stirred and moved by his words and prayers. Their hearts were so inflamed by his death that thousands joined him in his faith. So many declared themselves willing to die for their beliefs that the Scottish government re-examined their views on executing "heretics." After the death of Walter Milne, no one else was put to death for their faith in Scotland.

The Lord told the Apostle Paul, "My grace is enough for you. When you are weak, my power is made perfect

in you" (2 Corinthians 12:9 NCV). Walter Milne was living proof of this promise. The Spirit of God worked so miraculously in him, increasing his boldness and strength more and more until all who heard him knew his cause was just and true.

"We Are Only Here for a Few Days"

Mira Jarali
Mymensingh, Bangladesh
1997

The thirty Christian families stood in front of the mosque, surrounded by five hundred Muslims. "You'd better leave Christianity and become Muslim again," the crowd yelled. "If you do, we will help you. If not, we will beat you."

Mira Jarali and his family stood with the others. "We were all new converts from Islam, which makes them really angry," he said. "Second-generation Christians do not upset them as much."

On that morning, every believer, including women and children, had to stand before the Muslim leaders for four hours while each family was questioned. When Mira's turn came to stand before the court, he said, "In your religion there is no salvation, no hope for going to heaven. I have Jesus, and now I am whole. Now Jesus has forgiven my sins and I have hope for heaven."

Following the hearing, all of the Christian families were forbidden to get water from the village well. From that day on, they have had to walk and carry their water more than a mile every day. Then the villagers accused Mira and several others of stealing water. "The police beat me, kicked me, and put me in prison for thirty days. I was tied to the back of another Christian man. We were beaten for four days then locked in a cell with sixty Muslim prisoners."

The Muslim prisoners were sympathetic. "It is better that you are Christians," they told Mira. "It is a good life. Muslims are not at peace; they are always fighting each other."

Mira's land was confiscated by the village's Muslim leader, even though Mira's wife was expecting a baby. Members of his family have been beaten several times. When they walk through the village, people throw mud at them. The Christians have also been attacked in their little house church. Even though they are all new believers, they are not shaken by this harsh treatment.

"We give thanks to God that these things cannot destroy our spirit," Mira said. "Jesus told us that we are only here for a few days. We have eternal life and will stay with Him in heaven. He will take care of all of this."

We're not giving up. How could we! Even though on the outside it often looks like things are falling apart on us, on the inside, where God is making new life, not a day goes by without his unfolding grace. These hard times are small potatoes compared to the coming good times, the lavish celebration prepared for us. There's far more here than meets the eye. The things we see now are here today, gone tomorrow. But the things we can't see now will last forever.

Paul the Apostle
Martyred in Rome, AD 65
(2 CORINTHIANS 4:16-18
THE MESSAGE)

"Take the Oath"

Valya Vaschenko
12 years old
U.S.S.R.
1960s

Every eye in the room was upon Valya as the director of the school called her name again. "Valya Vaschenko," the director said firmly, "take the oath." Valya's mouth stayed shut tight. "Valya! say the oath," he commanded. "Valya... Very well, I will read it in your name."

Weeks earlier, the director of the school had decided that it was time that Valya, a twelve-year-old Christian girl in Russia, should become a member of the Communist children's group known as Pioneers. Valya refused, but refusal was not hers to make. By law, the director took the place of her parents.

When membership day came, the girls stood in a group before a table on which were laid the three-pointed, red Pioneer scarves. One by one the other girls had stepped forward to take the oath and put on a scarf. All but Valya.

As the director prepared to read the oath for Valya, he pointed to two other girls. "You will place the scarf on Valya's neck as I read."

He began, "I, a young Pioneer of the U.S.S.R., before my comrades — patriots deciding the question of my admission into the organization — promise that I shall stand firmly for the cause of Lenin and for the victory of Communism. I promise..."

But his next words were drowned out as Valya burst out in prayer to God and began to sing a hymn:

> "We will stand firm for the Gospel faith, for Christ, Following His example, forward all, forward after Him."

Again and again, in Russian schools, Christian children would stand up in class to pray out loud and to witness. These children were beaten and forced to leave their families, but others followed their example.

In 1963, prayer was banned in American public schools. What would have happened if American parents had taught their children not to submit to this decision? They would not have been beaten, and their parents would not have ended up in jail as in Russia.

In the United States, the First Amendment of the Constitution guarantees freedom of speech and freedom of religion. What has been done with that freedom? Must it be taken away as it was in Communist Russia or other dictatorial societies before any of us grows bold enough to stand up and proclaim Jesus before others?

WWJFD? What would a Jesus Freak do?

In Mainland China, a sword was put to the chest of a Christian. He was asked, "Are you a Christian?"

He answered, "Yes."

He would have been killed if an officer had not said, "Free him; he is an idiot."

Someone asked him later, "How could you confess Christ with such courage?"

He replied, "I had read the story of Peter's denial of Jesus, and I did not wish to weep bitterly."

Here is a true message: "If we died with Christ, we will live with him. If we don't give up, we will rule with him. If we deny that we know him, he will deny that he knows us. If we are not faithful, he will still be faithful. Christ cannot deny who he is."

Paul the Apostle
Martyred in Rome, AD 65
(2 TIMOTHY 2:11-13 CEV)

The Friends of Martyrs

Alice Driver and Alexander Gough
Ipswich, England
1557

"Let's get this over with," grumbled the sheriff. He had been walking most of the night, bringing the two Christians, Alice Driver and Alexander Gough, to Ipswich to be burned at the stake. It took longer than usual because such a great crowd of people had insisted on coming with them.

"First the hymns, now the prayers. I say they've been praying long enough," he told the bailiffs. "Get them up and chain them to the stakes."

When he heard this, Gough stood up and said to the sheriff, "Let us pray a little while longer, for we have a short time to live."

But the bailiff said, "Come on. Let's burn them!"

Gough answered, "Be careful, Sheriff. If you forbid our prayers, the vengeance of God hangs over your head."

Later, as the two were being fastened to the stake, some of their friends came and took them by the hands. Seeing this, the sheriff cried to his men, "Seize them! Don't let one of them escape."

When the crowd heard the sheriff's order and saw the danger those by the stake were in, they all ran towards it and crowded around the stake, hiding the friends of the martyrs.

When the sheriff saw this, he gave up and didn't arrest anyone. Then fire was put to the wood, and amid its flames these two heroic spirits passed beyond the reach of man's cruelty.

Don't ever forget those early days when you first learned about Christ. Remember how you remained faithful even though it meant terrible suffering. Sometimes you were exposed to public ridicule and were beaten, and sometimes you helped others who were suffering the same things.

You suffered along with those who were thrown into jail. When all you owned was taken from you, you accepted it with joy. You knew you had better things waiting for you in eternity.

Hebrews 10:32-34 NLT

"It Is Life That I Love"

Apollonius
Asia
AD 185

"The decree of man does not prevail over the decree of God," Apollonius boldly proclaimed to the Roman official who had just sentenced him to death. "The more you kill these innocent faithful, mocking justice and the laws, the more God will increase their number.

"We do not believe that it is hard to die for the true God. Everything that we are, we owe to Him, and we are ready to suffer anything to escape an end without honour. In life as in death we are the Lord's."

Perennis, the proconsul of Asia, then asked the Christian, "With such ideas, Apollonius, does death give you pleasure?"

"It is life that I love, Perennis, but this love does not make me fear death. For the life which I prefer to all else is eternal life, which awaits those who have lived faithfully in this world."

The proconsul was greatly moved by the words and conviction of Apollonius, but he chose his position and wealth over conversion. To show his mercy, though, he condemned Apollonius to beheading rather than the normal tortures and slow deaths generally reserved for Christians.

"I give my thanks to God, proconsul Perennis, with all those who confess the omnipotent God and Jesus Christ, His only Son, and the Holy Spirit, for the sentence you have just given and which brings me eternal life."

Where God's love is, there is no fear, because God's perfect love drives out fear.

John the Apostle
Tortured and exiled, AD 95
Roman Empire
(1 JOHN 4:18 NCV)

"I Devour Every Letter"

Pastor Lap Ma
Vietnam
1982

"I refuse to give you my church!" Pastor Lap Ma courageously faced the Communists. They came with guns and demanded that he sign papers that would have linked the Christian Missionary Alliance Church at Can Tho to the Communist party.

Lap Ma explained, "The Communists want to control pastors as their tool. Every month you must report what activities you are doing, who is the strongest Christian, who is sharing the Gospel, who is going to the army. You must become the police in your church."

The government was furious with his lack of cooperation. Since he was the leader of many pastors in other areas of Vietnam, the Communists made him an example, hoping that the pastors under him would decide to follow the government. Twenty-eight CMA pastors in that district wrote to the government about his case — and all were called to the police station and threatened.

Because he refused to cooperate, Lap Ma and his family were forced into exile by the government. Their clothing, books, letters, and property were confiscated. For twelve-and-a-half years, they were forced to live alone in remote areas on the Mekong Delta, unable to leave.

When Christians around the world heard of his arrest, many wrote letters, both to Pastor Lap Ma and to the government. Because of the international attention focused on his case, the police now allow him to leave his village and receive visitors — as long as he first gets their approval.

Pastor Lap Ma and his family have received over 3,000 letters from Christians around the world. Just knowing that someone is thinking of them encourages them for days.

"I devour every letter we receive and meditate on the Scriptures shared in them. I then share these words of encouragement and the Scriptures in Vietnamese with my family. We are glad and encouraged in spirit for the messages in them.

"I read these letters with prayers and tears, because I know our Father never will leave us nor forsake us. He has strengthened and helped us. Even in these years of great trial and persecution, my eleven children did not stop serving the Lord. All of them love the Lord and are serving the Lord full-time."

Lap Ma and his family remain in exile today.

Would you like to encourage a persecuted Christian family? Your letters can make a big difference in their lives. (Not all can write back. In some countries it can cost an entire week's wages to send a letter overseas!)

Or perhaps you would like to write a letter to the government on their behalf. These letters often mean the difference between life and death, jail or freedom for those who are persecuted for their faith.

For a copy of those currently in prison for their faith, write to The Voice of the Martyrs and ask for their monthly newsletter. For their address and information about what The Voice of the Martyrs is doing in the world today, look at the section about The Voice of the Martyrs in the back of this book.

The Courage of a Child

Siao-Mei
5 years old
Mainland China
During the Red Guard Era, 1966–69

Over and over, a mother spoke soothing words to her five-year-old child as they sat in their dark, damp cell. The woman was in jail because she had protested against the arrest of her bishop; her child was in jail because the little girl had nowhere else to go.

All the prisoners were indignant at seeing the child suffer so. Even the prison director said to the mother, "Don't you have pity on your daughter? Just declare that you give up being a Christian and will not go to church anymore. Then you and the child will be free."

In despair the woman agreed, and she was released. After two weeks, she was forced to shout from a stage before 10,000 people, "I am no longer a Christian." On their return home, the child, who had stood near her when she denied her faith, said, "Mummy, today Jesus is not satisfied with you."

The mother explained, "You wept in prison. I had to say this out of love for you."

Siao-Mei replied, "I promise that if we go to jail again for Jesus, I will not weep."

The mother ran to the prison director and told him, "You convinced me I should say wrong things for my daughter's sake, but she has more courage than I."

Both went back to prison. But Siao-Mei no longer wept.

I prayed to the Lord, and he answered me,

  freeing me from all my fears.

Those who look to him for help will be radiant with
  joy;

no shadow of shame will darken their faces.

Psalm 34:4,5 NLT

While in jail, we sang. Once the director
of the prison entered our cell, furious.
"I was told that you sing subversive songs
here. Let me hear one," he commanded.

We sang these moving words:

"O sacred Head, now wounded, with grief
and shame bowed down...."

He listened to the end, then turned and
left without saying a word. Later he
became a brother in the faith.

Richard Wurmbrand
Imprisoned for a total of 14 years
Romania
1940s, 50s, and 60s

O Sacred Head Now Wounded

Ascribed to St. Bernard of Clairvaux
1091-1153

O sacred Head, now wounded,
With grief and shame weighed down,
Now scornfully surrounded
With thorns, thine only crown;
O sacred Head, what glory,
What bliss till now was thine!
Yet, though despised and gory,
I joy to call thee mine.

How art thou pale with anguish,
With sore abuse and scorn;
How does that visage languish,
Which once was bright as morn!
Thy grief and bitter passion
Were all for sinners' gain;
Mine, mine was the transgression,
But thine the deadly pain.

What language shall I borrow
To thank thee, dearest friend,
For this thy dying sorrow,
Thy pity without end?
O make me thine forever,
And should I fainting be,
Lord, let me never, never
Outlive my love to Thee.

Be near when I am dying
O show thy Cross to me!
And, for my succour flying,
Come, Lord, to set me free.
These eyes, new faith receiving,
From Thee shall never move;
For he who dies believing
Dies safely in Thy love.

Amen.

Reversing a Denial

James Abbeys
England

1555

James Abbeys, a young Christian, wandered from place to place to avoid being arrested for practising his faith. In time, Abbeys was captured and brought before the Bishop of Norwich, who threatened him with prison and death. He promised Abbeys freedom if only he would deny his faith. Finally Abbeys gave in to the pressure. He was released and was about to leave the bishop when they called him back and gave him a bag of money.

Once outside, Abbeys' conscience bothered him terribly. He knew his actions had displeased the Lord, so he immediately returned to the bishop. He threw the money at him and declared that he was sorry he'd denied his faith and accepted the gift. The bishop and his men started again to work on Abbeys with their threats and promises, but this time Abbeys did not give in. He stood firm, and as a result he was burned at the stake.

Two people denied Jesus the night before His death: Judas and Peter. Both wept for their mistake. What was the difference between the two? Judas turned away from

God and judged himself. Peter repented, went back to God, and let Him forgive and restore him.

Never underestimate the power of Jesus to forgive and restore.

God doesn't take back the gifts he has given or forget about the people he has chosen.

> Paul the Apostle
> Beheaded in Rome, AD 65
> (ROMANS 10:29 CEV)

Reading the Walls

Robert J. Thomas
Korea
1866

When he heard the shouts, Robert J. Thomas looked up from reading his Bible. Korean soldiers were boarding the ship, waving long, flashing knives. When he saw that he was going to be killed, he held out the Korean Bible to them saying, "Jesus, Jesus." His head was cut off.

Robert J. Thomas, the first missionary to Korea, survived only a few months in that country. He had been ordained on June 4, 1863, at a little church in Hanover, Wales. He and his wife left for Korea in July, sent by the London Mission Society. His wife died soon after arriving at Shanghai, China.

Thomas went on alone to Korea, where he began to learn the language and evangelize. In 1866, Thomas rode the American ship, *The General Sherman*, along the Taedong River (where the capital of North Korea is today). When the *Sherman* ran aground on a sandbar, the Korean soldiers on shore became suspicious, boarded the ship, and killed the foreigners, including Thomas.

Twenty-five years after Thomas' death, someone discovered a little guest house in this area with some strange wallpaper. The paper had Korean characters printed on it. The owner of the house explained that he had used the pages of a book to paste on the wall to preserve the writing. Not only the owner, but many of the guests would come in and stay to read the walls — to read the pages of the Bible Thomas had given to his murderers.

Even though North Korea is now ruled by Communists, the church lives. The work of Robert J. Thomas, the short-lived missionary, continues. Today, more than one hundred Christian families secretly worship Jesus Christ in this area. God's Word has gone from being hidden inside their walls to being hidden inside their hearts.

Many would call Thomas' years of preparation a waste. He worked so long for only three brief months in which he did not even convert one person, and it cost him and his wife their lives. But God can always take what seems like failure and turn it into success. Though Thomas died before saving anyone, he penetrated the darkness of that land with the Word of God. The Word Thomas deposited there created a pocket of light that perseveres today.

When you were a child, you might have sat on a small stool and looked at your mother's embroidery. From your point of view, it was a confusion of zigzags, knots, and loose threads. Then your mother, to help you understand, turned the embroidery on the right side so you could see and appreciate the design.

You must stop looking on the wrong side of things.... Lift your hearts to heavenly places and look down upon events from that vantage point. You will see life's temporary sufferings as a gathering of pearls and jewels with which we will be adorned in eternity.

Richard Wurmbrand
Imprisoned for a total of 14 years
Romania
1940s, 50s, and 60s

Standing Unafraid

Peruvian Congregation
Cano, Peru
1991

Terrorists had killed their pastor the night before. His body was on the floor under a blanket with some candles around it. Terrorists had also burned the church and seventeen houses — all belonging to Christians.

The people had no more church, no more pastor, no more houses. Yet, they continued to gather together fearlessly, about thirty of them. They stood in the muddy street to have their song service.

Stand united, singular in vision, contending for people's trust in the Message, the good news, not flinching or dodging in the slightest before the opposition. Your courage and unity will show them what they're up against: defeat for them, victory for you — and both because of God.

Paul the Apostle
Martyred in Rome, AD 65
(PHILIPPIANS 1:27,28 THE MESSAGE)

"Note Our Faces Well"

Perpetua, Saturas, and Felicitas
Carthage, North Africa
AD 202

Six Christians climbed up on the judgment platform. Below them, a vast crowd had gathered in the marketplace to watch their trial. One by one, the others were questioned and confessed their faith. As soon as it was Perpetua's turn, she saw her aged father holding her infant child in his arms.

"Have pity on your baby," he begged.

The judge took up her father's cause. "Spare your father's white hairs, spare the tender years of your child. Offer a sacrifice for the welfare of the Emperor."

Perpetua answered, "I will not sacrifice."

"Are you a Christian?" the judge demanded.

"I am a Christian," was her answer.

The judge passed sentence: Perpetua and her fellow Christians were all condemned to be killed by wild beasts as a show for the crowd on Caesar's birthday. Five of the six were new converts, the other, Saturus, was the one who had first told them about Jesus. Saturus had not been there when the others were arrested, but when he heard about it, he turned himself in and joined them in prison.

During their stay in prison, they continually told others about their faith. The day before the games, as the prisoners had their last meal, a crowd gathered. The believers spoke to the crowd with their usual courage, threatening them with the judgment of God, calling to witness their happiness at giving their lives.

Saturus said, "Note our faces well, that you may recognize us on the Day of Judgment." The pagans left the prison surprised at their peace and joy in the face of death. Later many became believers themselves.

On the day before she was to die, Perpetua had a vision from God, which she recorded with her own hand:

"I saw Pomponius the deacon come to the door of the prison and knock loudly.... He was wearing a white robe without a belt, with strange shoes on his feet. He said, 'Perpetua, we are waiting for you. Come.'

"I saw a huge crowd watching eagerly. And because I knew that I was condemned to fight the beasts, I was amazed that no beasts were let loose on me. Then a mean-looking Egyptian came out with his attendants to fight against me. At the same time handsome young men came to me to be my attendants and supporters....

"And a man came out, amazingly tall, so that he rose above the top of the amphitheatre, wearing a purple robe...and with strange shoes made of gold and silver on his feet; he carried a wand like a trainer, and a green bough with golden apples on it. He asked for silence and said: 'If this Egyptian prevails over this woman, he shall kill her with a sword; and if she prevails over him, she shall receive this bough.' Then he left.

"We approached one another and began to use our fists. My opponent wanted to catch hold of my feet, but I kept on kicking his face with my heels. Suddenly I was lifted up into the air and began to kick him like someone who no longer walked on earth. But when I saw that the fight was by no means over, I joined my two hands, linking the fingers of the one with the fingers of the other. And I caught hold of his head and he fell on his face; and I walked on his head.

"The people began to shout and my supporters started to sing psalms. I came forward to the trainer and was given the bough. He kissed me and said to me, 'Peace be with you, my daughter.' Proud of my triumph, I began to go to the gate of life.

"At that moment I awoke. And I perceived that I would not be fighting with beasts but with the devil. But I knew that the victory was mine."

That night, Saturus also had a vision. He wrote:

"We began to be carried eastwards by four angels whose hands did not touch us.... And when we were clear of the world below, we saw a great light, and I said to Perpetua, 'This is what the Lord promised us. We have received His promise.'

"We came upon a great open space, which was rather like a garden, with rose trees and all kinds of flowers.... In the garden were four angels who were more glorious than the others. When they saw us, they paid homage and said to the other angels, 'Here they are; here they are.' Trembling, the four angels which were carrying us set us down....

"We came near to a palace the walls of which were built as it were of light, and before the gate of that place four angels were standing. As we entered, they clothed us in white robes. We went in and heard a sound as of one voice saying, 'Holy, holy, holy' without ceasing. And we saw sitting in the same place One...with hair as white as snow and with the face of a youth....

"As we entered we stood in wonder before the throne, and the four angels lifted us up, and we kissed Him, and He stroked our faces with His hand.

"We went out...and we began to recognize many brethren there, martyrs too amongst them. We were all fed on a fragrance beyond telling, which contented us. Then in my joy I awoke."

The day of their victory dawned, and the martyrs went from the prison to the amphitheatre as if they were on their way to heaven. Their faces were radiant. Perpetua followed at a gentle pace, as a great lady of Christ. The power of her gaze forced the spectators to lower their eyes. She sang a hymn of triumph.

At the beginning of the show, two of the men were attacked by a leopard and then mauled by a bear. A wild boar was then let loose on Saturus, but the boar turned on the one who unleashed him, goring him in the stomach. Saturus was only dragged on the sand. Then he was tied up on the bridge in front of a bear, but the bear refused to come out of his den. So for the second time Saturus was left unhurt.

Perpetua and a young woman named Felicitas were put in the arena with a bull. Felicitas fell, seriously wounded. Perpetua was tossed in the air, and her robe was torn. As soon as she got up, she ran to Felicitas and gently raised her from the ground. When the bull refused to attack them again, they were removed from the arena.

The show was almost over; Saturus was put in the arena one last time, the leopard was let loose, and with one bite, Saturus was mortally wounded.

Finally, those who were still alive were brought back in to be killed by gladiators. First, they gave one another the kiss of peace. Then all remained still and received the sword in silence.

Perpetua was assigned a young, untried gladiator, who was not used to such scenes of violence. He stabbed her weakly several times between the ribs, but did not kill her, so Perpetua guided his wavering hand to her throat.

Perpetua had it all: noble birth, wealth, a fine family, education, intelligence, youth, and beauty. But none of these things, not even her love for her baby, compared to her love for Jesus. Obeying His will for her life was her first priority. She was a Jesus Freak!

She wrote these final words to her family:

Do not be ashamed by my death. I think it is the greatest honour of my life and thank God for calling me to give my life for His sake and in His cause. He gave the same honour to the holy prophets, His dearly beloved apostles, and His blessed, chosen martyrs. I have no doubt that I am dying for God's cause and the cause of truth.

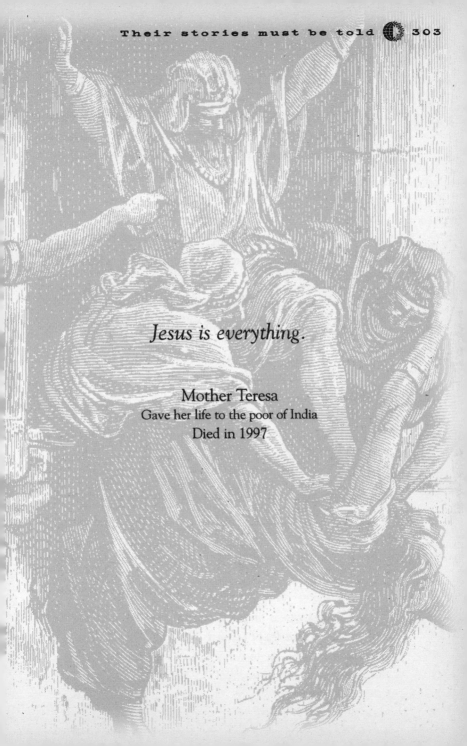

Jesus is everything.

Mother Teresa
Gave her life to the poor of India
Died in 1997

Commanded to Preach

Boian
Romania
1964

The day the Adventist pastor Boian of Ploiesti was released from prison, a Communist officer asked him, "What will you do now?"

Boian replied, "I will begin my Christian work, with or without your permission, exactly where I left off when you arrested me."

He kept his word and eventually appeared before the court again. The Communist judge asked him, "Do you regret having preached illegally?"

"Why do you have stupid laws that forbid what is pleasing to the Lord? If you apply them, God will punish you here and in eternity."

"You were not allowed by us to preach."

"God not only allowed me to preach, but commanded me to do so. Read the order yourself in the Bible. You will find it in Matthew 28:19,20."

He was sentenced to eight years in prison. He already had three years of jail behind him.

Such fearlessness is an excellent food for souls. As we look at these examples of courage and upon Jesus Christ who inspired them, we too are changed into a new breed of Christian — into Jesus Freaks!

"I Am a Christian"

Blandina
France
AD 172

The tormentors had been taking turns torturing the Christian woman in every way from morning till evening. At last, they collapsed in exhaustion. "We have tried everything on this one," said the older of the two. "I can't think of anything else to do to her."

"How can she still be alive? Any one of the tortures we have used today should have been enough to kill her. Yet we used everything, and she still lives!"

Blandina, like many martyrs, had been tormented by the thought that she might not be able to endure the pain and might deny Jesus. But she was so steadfast in all her sufferings, she was filled with so much power, that even those who tortured her in relays all day long were faint and weary.

Every time she repeated her confession: "I am a Christian," her heart was strengthened, so she was able to endure the pain.

After all this torture, she was returned to prison to wait for the next holiday, when she and other Christians would appear before the crowds in the stadium. There, she was beaten and roasted upon a red-hot metal plate. Then she was wound up in a net and thrown before bulls, which tossed her many times high up with their horns, and then let her fall down again. Even with all this, she was still alive!

Finally, the judge commanded that she be killed with the sword.

*Lord God, these men take away my life full of misery,
but You will give me life everlasting.*

Maurice Blanc
Martyred in Merindol
1547

A Most Excellent Map

John Bunyan
England
1660

"I will let you go, if you promise not to preach." The judge looked down from his bench at John Bunyan, the tinker-preacher.

"Sir," the Christian replied, "I will stay in prison till the moss grows on my eyelids rather than disobey God!"

"Then I hereby sentence you to six years in the Bedford jail."

God had given Bunyan a powerful preaching gift and a great ability to touch the hearts of men. Although he wasn't well-educated — he was forced to leave school at an early age to help his father work — he could read. While in prison, Bunyan read two books, the *King James Bible* and John Foxe's *Book of Martyrs*, and preached to his fellow prisoners. He gained a new awareness of the truth of Scripture and of the presence of Jesus Christ, declaring:

"Jesus Christ also was never more real and apparent than now: Here I have seen Him and felt Him indeed."

During his imprisonment, he also began to write. He wrote many books and tracts, including the story of his conversion, *Grace Abounding to the Chiefest of Sinners*. As soon as he was released, Bunyan started preaching again, and within just a few weeks, he was back in jail. Six years later, the King of England suspended the laws against the Nonconformists, and Bunyan was released.

By now, he was in great demand as a preacher. He frequently visited London, where he preached to large congregations. Sometimes as many as 1,200 people would attend a service at 7 o'clock on a winter morning. On Sundays, the meeting house could not hold all who wanted to hear him, and hundreds were turned away.

After three short years, the King of England changed his mind and began persecuting Nonconformists again. Bunyan was sent to jail for the third time. While in prison, this Jesus Freak began writing a book that helped thousands of believers for centuries to come. *Pilgrim's Progress*, the first novel ever written, is the story of a dream in which Christian journeys from the City of Destruction to the Celestial City. Some have called it "the most excellent map to be found anywhere."

Today it continues to be one of the best-known Christian books of all time and has been translated into hundreds of languages. When China's Communist government printed *Pilgrim's Progress* as an example of Western cultural heritage, an initial printing of 200,000 copies was sold out in three days!

He who would valiant be 'gainst all disaster,
Let him in constancy follow the Master.
There's no discouragement shall make him once
    relent
His first avowed intent to be a pilgrim.
Since, Lord, Thou dost defend us with Thy Spirit,
We know we at the end shall life inherit.

Then fancies flee away! I'll fear not what men say,
I'll labour night and day to be a pilgrim.

Hymn by John Bunyan

The Orthodox Bishop Andrew of Ufa
was sentenced to death. The story is told
that before the execution, he asked to be
allowed to pray. As he knelt, he
simply was no more. The henchmen were
in a panic, knowing they would lose
their lives if he disappeared. After an hour
he reappeared on his knees, in prayer,
surrounded by a luminous cloud.
The sentence was carried out,
but one of the henchmen was converted
and told the story.

A Supernatural Release

Peter
Jerusalem, Israel
AD 44

The believers met secretly in homes, fearing public gatherings. Many had been harassed, persecuted, and arrested because they were followers of Jesus of Nazareth.

As they prepared for their Easter celebrations, word came that one of their leaders, James the brother of John, had been arrested and beheaded. The believers were overwhelmed at the swiftness of the execution. Even more alarming was the public acceptance of such brutality. There was no tolerance for this new sect that proclaimed Jesus as the Messiah.

Another church leader was taken into custody. To ensure that no one came to his rescue, two soldiers stood on guard within his small cell, each bound to the prisoner at the wrist. Two additional guards were ordered to stand watch outside the cell. Instead of being immediately executed like the first, he was to be held in custody until after the Passover celebration, when he was to be executed publicly.

The believers gathered on behalf of their imprisoned leader and began to pray fervently, asking God to deliver him from such a fate. Word spread throughout the region, and within a matter of hours, thousands committed themselves to pray.

The night before his scheduled execution, the condemned man received a visitor. An angel of the Lord appeared and the apostle Peter was miraculously released from prison. The others were so surprised by his quick release, that when he knocked at their door, they would not let him in because they didn't believe it was him!

Soon after that Herod died and Peter remained in Jerusalem as a leader of the church for some time.

AD 65

From the early Christian historian Hegesippus, we learn that Peter eventually travelled to Rome to minister in his old age. Nero determined to have him executed, but the disciples there heard about it and urged Peter to flee. Though resistant at first, Peter eventually gave in, but as he approached the city gate, he saw Jesus walking in the other direction.

Peter fell to his knees and said, "Lord, where are You going?"

Jesus answered, "I've come to be crucified again."

Peter took this to mean that it was his time to die just as Jesus had prophesied to him in John 21:19, so he returned to the city. Upon being captured and sentenced to be crucified, Peter announced that he was not worthy to be crucified in the same position as his Saviour, and requested to die on the cross upside down. The Romans honoured this request.

I shall always be ready to remind you of these things, even though you already know them, and have been established in the truth which is present with you. And I consider it right, as long as I am in this earthly dwelling,

to stir you up by way of reminder, knowing that the laying aside of my earthly dwelling is imminent, as also our Lord Jesus Christ has made clear to me.

> Peter the Apostle
> Written three years before his
> death
> (2 PETER 1:12-14 NAS)

Peter knew that one day he would face death for following Jesus, because Jesus had told him he would. Yet Peter never flinched from the call to follow Him anywhere, and he urged all believers to do the same. Like Paul, Peter was delivered from death again and again until he had finished the course God had laid out for him. When it was finished, Jesus was there to welcome him home.

Unashamed

Well, how much more do I need to say? It would take too long to recount the stories of the faith of Gideon, Barak, Samson, Jephthah, David, Samuel, and all the prophets. By faith these people overthrew kingdoms, ruled with justice, and received what God had promised them. They shut the mouths of lions, quenched the flames of fire, and escaped death by the edge of the sword. Their weakness was turned to strength. They became strong in battle and put whole armies to flight. Women received their loved ones back again from death.

But others trusted God and were tortured, preferring to die rather than turn from God and be free. They placed their hope in the resurrection to a better life. Some were mocked, and their backs were cut open with whips. Others were chained in dungeons. Some died by stoning, and some were sawed in half; others killed with the sword....

Therefore, since we are surrounded by such a huge crowd of witnesses to the life of faith, let us strip off every weight that slows us down, especially sin that so easily hinders our progress. And let us run with endurance the race that God has set before us. We do this by keeping our eyes on Jesus, on whom our faith depends from start to finish.

Hebrews 11:32-37; 12:1,2 NLT

from this day forward...

I **will** make a difference.
Jesus, I thank You that You **suffered**
and died for me on the cross to pay for my sins.

Father, I thank You that You raised Jesus
from the dead to be my **living** Lord and Saviour.
Holy Spirit, I thank You that You will lead me

to do the right thing and change my world.

Today, Lord, I want to make You a promise.
I **will** not **be ashamed** of Your name
or Your Gospel.
I **will** do what I can for those who are
persecuted and pray for them.
I **will** look enemies in the eye and love
them with Your love. I will pray for them and
love them — no matter what the
consequences.
I **will** follow Your voice wherever You lead
me, unafraid, for I know You will be with me.

If I should stumble, if I fall, if I should
deny Your name, if I should feel guilty that I
did not pray or forgot to do something
You've asked me to do,

I **will** not **quit.** I will not wallow
in guilt. I will turn back to You, confess my sin,
and do what You called me to do, because that is
why You died for me.
I **will** s t a n d   w i t h   Y o u
and my brothers and sisters around the world,
because no matter what happens, no

matter what I face or how it looks, in the end, we
will be **victorious** — we will inherit eternity and
heaven with You.   I can do nothing else, b e c a u s e

...I am a Jesus Freak.

SIGNATURE   DAY

Persecution in the World Today...

AFGHANISTAN

Afghanistan is no stranger to struggle. The Soviet invasion in 1978 brought disaster, but their pullout a decade later did not bring peace. When the Communists lost power, Muslims took their place and engaged in a civil war — an Islamic jihad or holy war. This jihad degenerated into a cruel contest for religious and political supremacy between Islamic factions. The Afghani people are left to pick up the shattered pieces of their lives. The Taliban leadership set up stringent rules — women are not allowed to attend school or hold jobs, and men must adhere to a strict Islamic code in which they all have beards. Non-Muslims are denied freedom of assembly, and open profession of faith in Jesus Christ has often led to death. There are still 88 unreached people groups in this nation. Pray that abuses by the Taliban regime will cause many to seek God's grace.

ALGERIA

For more than thirty years Algeria has been ruled by a one-party socialist regime backed by a strong army. The prospect of a new government, while possible, would likely lead only to a new tyranny, since the opposition consists primarily of Muslim revivalists. This polarized situation could lead to civil war. In recent years, Algerian Christians have suffered a reign of violence from the Islamic Salvation Front. Members of this Muslim rebel group have been known to march through towns and slit the throats of anyone who has not lived up to their call to Islamic fundamentalism. Two-thirds of Algerians are so young that they have known nothing but the confusion of the socialist system. Algeria has very few Christians and the church is suffering discouragement. Social pressures often lead Christian girls to marry Muslims, and some believers withdraw from fellowship due to intimidation from family, friends, and Muslim extremists. Pray that the Lord will raise up true believers in Algeria to be a light among its people.

AZERBAIJAN

Azerbaijan has been dominated by its neighbours for centuries. Subject to the U.S.S.R. during most of the 20th century, Azerbaijan broke away from the Soviet bloc in 1991. The Christian population is almost entirely Armenian and Russian. Many fled the country following a massacre of their people in 1989. While Azerbaijan offers official guarantees of religious freedom, the nationalists are becoming more Islamic and anti-Christian. Armenian churches have been closed and few of the Christians left in Azerbaijan would feel secure enough to attend if they reopened. There is one bright spot — literature can be freely printed and has been eagerly received, but with such a small percentage of Christians, distribution is limited. Pray that God raises up more servants to distribute Christian literature to the people of this nation.

BANGLADESH

Bangladesh is continually plagued by disaster. Almost half of this country consists of low-lying islands, most of them less than nine feet above sea level. This geography causes a huge loss of life during the country's frequent floods and cyclones, such as happened in the summer of 1998. Although Bangladesh is a democracy, corruption and eighteen coup attempts during the last quarter century have left their scars. An Islamic state since 1988, Bangladesh is currently experiencing the rise of a more radical interpretation of Islam which threatens Christian work and witness. Believers are often denied access to public water wells by Muslim extremists, and many have been forced from their homes and beaten by Muslim mobs. These extremists have also destroyed rickshaws owned by Christians, thereby taking their only source of income. Pray that Bangladesh will be flooded with Jesus Christ's love.

BHUTAN

This underdeveloped country is moving out of feudalism towards a constitutional monarchy. Bhutan was isolated from the outside world until the Communist takeover of China in 1949 forced the country to stop doing business exclusively with Tibet. Christian witness was tightly restricted until 1965. The country stayed open for over two decades until it became obvious that Christianity was making headway. Since a new restrictive atmosphere has taken hold, missions have been allowed to operate only in humanitarian projects, and on the condition that they do not evangelize. Since Bhutan's greatest problem — leprosy — has been nearly eradicated, missions are scrambling for other reasons to stay. Some Bhutanese are coming to Christ due to the witness of Indian believers visiting Bhutan. All public worship and evangelism by non-Buddhists are illegal in Bhutan. In April 1997, a pastor who preached openly among the mountain tribal people was arrested, thrown in prison, and tortured, causing severe head injuries. He died ten days after his release. A prominent local politician lost his job because of his Christian activities. One of Bhutan's greatest needs is a Bible in the Dzongkha language. Pray for workers to translate God's Word for the Dzongkha people.

BRUNEI

Brunei's 1959 constitution called for a monarchy with five advisory councils, but in 1962 the Sultan assumed emergency powers during a rebellion and has retained them since. He installed relatives as advisors and declared Brunei an Islamic state. Constitutional guarantees of the free practice of religion are steadily eroding. Christian leaders were expelled in 1991, and the following year Christian literature was banned and the celebration of Christmas outlawed. Muslims are adding to their numbers from local tribes and immigrants, and they control the nation's education system. Conversion to Christianity is restricted since it is illegal to evangelize Muslims. Pray for the Sultan of Brunei to meet the King of kings.

MAINLAND CHINA

Chairman Mao Zedong declared China to be the communist People's Republic of China in 1949 and quickly sought to purge society of anything religious, causing China's people to endure great hardship ever since. Mao's Great Leap Forward in the late 1950s and the Cultural Revolution in the 1960s and 1970s left millions of his countrymen dead or victimized. Today, Chinese Christians have increased freedom, however in some regions they still experience tremendous persecution. With its policies of forced abortion and sterilization, China's human rights record is still among the worst in the world. Authorities reportedly sell the organs of executed prisoners to meet the demand for transplants. Its system of "re-education through labour" detains hundreds of thousands each year in work camps without even a court hearing.

China's "strike-hard" policy, presented as a crackdown on criminals, is hardest on Christians, putting more believers in prison or under detention than in any other country. The confiscation of church property and Bibles continues — even Bibles officially printed by the government. Yet the Church grows: an estimated 3,000 Chinese come to Christ each day. China's house church movement, which comprises approximately 90 per cent of China's Christians, endures unimaginable persecution, yet stands on its commitment to preach the Gospel no matter the cost. In 1998, house church leaders for the first time publicly called on the Communist government to officially recognize house churches. Pray for continued faithfulness of Chinese believers.

COMORO ISLANDS

The Comoro Islands gained their independence from France in 1975. Since then they have been plagued with seventeen attempted coups, including invasions from France. In October 1997, a new constitution was approved by 85 per cent of the voters. Unfortunately, this new document greatly increased the influence of Islam. Public witness by Christians is now forbidden, and believers are not permitted to meet openly. Pray for blessings for Christians who continue to meet in secret despite laws restricting such gatherings.

CUBA

In 1959, Fidel Castro came to power threatening Cubans with socialism or death. In the mid 1960s, Castro labelled Catholics and Protestants "social scum" and forced both lay people and clergy into labour camps under inhumane conditions. Cuba's constitution was amended in 1992 to guarantee freedom of religion. But today, despite the government's claims of religious freedom, Christians who evangelize are imprisoned and churches are destroyed. In 1996, the Ministry of Justice ordered the closure of all house churches, estimated to number between 3,000 and 10,000. Thankfully, most churches did not comply and continue to influence Cuba for Christ. In early 1999, thousands of imported Bibles were burned by Cuban soldiers. This was the third known mass burning of Bibles since Castro took power. Pray that Fidel Castro will come to a saving knowledge of Jesus Christ.

CYPRUS

A British-controlled state until 1960, the country has now been split into Greek and Turkish communities. This long-standing political situation is in dire need of resolution. According to *Operation World*, more Mormons and Jehovah's Witnesses live on the island than evangelicals. Cyprus has only a handful of missionaries, and they face opposition. In the Turkish North, where almost everyone is Muslim, no active witness is tolerated and the church is limited to a few small groups of believers. Pray that believers will experience the empowerment of the Holy Spirit to share the Gospel, and that the love of Jesus Christ will break down ethnic barriers.

EGYPT

During the early centuries after Jesus Christ, Egypt was predominantly Christian. In AD 969, the country was conquered by Jawhar al-Siqilli and Cairo founded as the new capital, but thankfully Egypt's Coptic Christian Church never disappeared. Today, Egypt has the Middle East's largest Christian community. However, the country's constitution gives preference to Muslims and Christians are treated as second-class citizens, denied political representation, and discriminated against in employment. The government uses an 1856 Ottoman Empire law to keep any church from being built, repaired, or even repainted without the permission of Egypt's president. Christians are also susceptible to attacks by Muslim extremists, who often go unpunished by Egyptian authorities. In February 1997, Muslim militants murdered fifteen Christians inside their place of worship. In August 1998, two Egyptian Christians in the village of Al-Kosheh were found murdered. Reliable reports show that 1,200 Christian villagers were detained during the criminal investigation that followed while Muslim villagers were largely left alone. Egyptian police subjected the citizens to brutal beatings. Women and girls were stripped naked, threatened with rape, and tortured with electric shocks to their genitals in the presence of their male family members. The Egyptian government, despite stating their policies to protect minority religious believers, took no action to punish the security officers involved in ordering and carrying out the torture. In October 1998, the St. Arsanius Coptic Orthodox Church was reopened by President Hosni Mubarak after being closed by the government in July. Pray that Mubarak's heart will be softened towards Christians and that more churches will be allowed to reopen.

EQUATORIAL GUINEA

After 190 years under Spanish rule, Equatorial Guinea emerged in 1969 as a dictatorship under Marcias Nguema. The following decade brought an incredible weight of oppression upon the people. With help from Russian Soviets, Nguema murdered tens of thousands of people. A military coup in 1979 brought about a one-party presidential government. Before independence from Spain, Equatorial Guinea was one of the most prosperous countries of West Africa, but it has turned into one of the poorest. Church leaders were forced to succumb to government pressure or suffer. Sadly, many succumbed to this pressure. Today, open witness is banned and no new church denominations are approved. There are few missionaries, and *Operation World* reports only 25 trained pastors in the whole nation. Pray that God will raise up spiritual leaders for this nation.

INDONESIA

This collection of 13,500 islands was the site of one of the few failures of a Communist movement to overthrow a government. In 1965, tensions built to a showdown between Communists and Muslims. When the Muslims emerged victorious, over half a million Communist sympathizers were killed, and many others came to Christ. In 1998 student-led protests brought about the resignation of President Suharto, bringing to power his hand-picked successor, Jusuf Habibie. During the upheaval, many Chinese Christians had their homes and shops raided and burned, and many were beaten, raped, and killed. The government forces people to carry an identification card that includes their religious status. The government promotes a belief called Pancasila — meaning that all may choose to follow Christianity, Islam, Buddhism, or Hinduism — but Muslims receive preferential treatment. The political strength of Islam is used to limit evangelism and reduce Christian influence on public life. Since early 1996, rioting mobs of Muslim extremists have burned or destroyed over fifty church buildings, killing several Christians. Pray that the Holy Spirit will burn in the hearts of believers, and that others will come to know Jesus Christ.

IRAN

The overthrow of the Shah in 1979 ended Iran's friendship with the West and installed a Shiite Muslim government set on crushing any deviating faith. Today, persecution persists despite constitutional guarantees of religious freedom. Life is not easy for Iranian Christians — open witness is banned and the government has sent spies to monitor Christian groups. Believers are also discriminated against in education, employment, and property ownership. In the last five years, several pastors have been murdered. Missions are not allowed to enter Iran, but a growing number of Muslims have converted to Christianity. There are also possibilities of evangelizing the millions of Iranians who live abroad, including more than two million in the United States. Ask the Lord to give Christians creative ways to share the Gospel inside Iran.

IRAQ

Iraq has experienced a troubled history since Bible times. This is the land where the Jews were taken into exile, and the prophet Daniel served the kings of Babylon. Since Saddam Hussein came to power in 1979, there has been only more turmoil for the people of Iraq. Most of the 1980s were spent at war with Iran over control of the Shatt-al-Arab waterway to the Persian Gulf. The subsequent Persian Gulf War was followed by genocide of select ethnic groups. Tens of thousands, including Christians, were gassed, shot, or forced to leave their homes. The government's repressive power and military might remain in the clutches of Hussein. Religions are accepted if they show loyalty to his regime, and the importing of Christian literature is restricted. Pray that Saddam Hussein will bend his knee to the Lord, causing many to surrender their lives to Jesus Christ.

KUWAIT

This gulf state is best known in the U.S. as the catalyst for the 1991 Gulf War in which Kuwait was liberated from Iraq. Kuwait is the only gulf nation to hold legislative elections, but the real power has been held by the al-Sabath family for the last two centuries. Sunni Islam is the state religion. Although the Gulf War resulted in loosening strict religious rules in Kuwait, full freedom of worship is still not a reality. Only Muslims may become citizens. Christians have the freedom to live and work in Kuwait, but worship must be within the Christian community (a physical location). Evangelism to Kuwaitis is forbidden. The Christian community in Kuwait includes 27 congregations that conduct church meetings in many languages. The government discourages Christianity by providing financial incentives for those who claim to be Muslim and has purchased large quantities of Bibles in order to burn them. Pray that God raises a standard of justice and righteousness on behalf of Christians in Kuwait.

LAOS

In 1975 the Communist Pathet Lao took over this land and established a one-party state under the Lao People's Revolutionary Party. Although Laos is rich with natural resources and has great potential for foreign investment, growth is hampered by the socialist government's slow reforms. Eighty-five per cent of the people are subsistence farmers. Today, the three or four Christian churches in the capital city of Vientiane are considered potentially subversive and are closely monitored by the government. House church meetings are raided and Lao Christians are arrested, while foreign Christians are expelled. Communist leaders in some districts have implemented a programme called "New Mechanism," in which anyone who does not convert to Buddhism or animism is forcibly removed from their district. Pray for salvation among Communist Party members.

LIBYA

Since 1969, Muammar al-Qaddafi has single-handedly ruled Libya. This dictator is perhaps best known for his association with other radical regimes and terrorist groups. But even Qaddafi is legitimately concerned about the growing threat of Islamists in his country. For this reason, he has attempted to appease Muslims by broadening Islamic law. Qaddafi shields his countrymen from all outside influence, making evangelism difficult. Christian literature may enter only through secretive means. There are very few Libyan believers. Almost all Christians are foreign workers, and their meetings are strictly monitored by the government. Ask the Lord to open Qaddafi's eyes to what Islam really is.

MALAYSIA

This federation of thirteen states was formed in 1963 as a monarchy. Malaysia's constitution guarantees religious freedom, but fundamentalist Muslims do everything in their power politically to inhibit Christian evangelism. All Christian literature printed must be for non-Malays only. Ethnic Malays are not allowed to have a Christian place of worship. The Indonesian Bible and several other Christian books containing certain phrases common to Islam have been banned by the government to prevent the unauthorized use of religious terms. Permits for building churches are rarely granted and house churches are strongly discouraged. Freedom of speech and public assembly are also restricted. Pray for the effective ministry of Western Christians living in Malaysia.

MALDIVES

This 500-mile-long string of 1,200 islands in the Indian Ocean is considered one of the least evangelized nations on earth. The president, who under the constitution must be a male Sunni Muslim, is appointed by the Parliament. Free speech is not respected for the press or for non-Muslim religions. In 1998, all known Christian foreigners were expelled from the country, and all known Maldivian Christians were arrested. The Muslim government is committed to strengthening Islam to preserve national unity. Ask the Lord to raise up Christian leaders in the Maldives.

MAURITANIA

Mauritania is one of the most restricted nations in the world. Mauritanians have had to endure much hardship recently with long droughts and ethnic squabbling. Freedom of religion is non-existent in this state, where Islam has dominated for over 1,000 years and only one-fifth of one percent of the population is Christian. It is illegal for citizens to enter non-Muslim households, and anyone who confesses Jesus Christ faces the death penalty under the law. People who have simply shown interest in the Gospel have found themselves tortured and imprisoned. Christian literature and religious radio broadcasts are not allowed. Pray that, despite restrictions, Mauritanian believers will find freedom in Jesus Christ.

MOROCCO

Islam entered Morocco in the 7th century through invading Arab armies. Today, Morocco's king, Hasson II, is committed to the preservation of Islam as the religion of all Moroccans. He even claims to be a direct descendant of the prophet Mohammed. Morocco is a hostile environment for Christians, as anyone who comes to Jesus Christ can face charges of treachery and illegal contact with foreign missions. Many have endured ostracism from their families, loss of employment, and imprisonment for their faith. Missionary work is not permitted, but many foreign Christians are working in secular roles, hoping to quietly win souls to Christ. Pray that, through the work of those who have counted the cost to follow Christ, many will come to know the Lord.

MYANMAR (Burma)

Since it was invaded by Japan in 1942, Burma has been well acquainted with struggle. Renamed Myanmar by the current regime, this union of seven districts and seven ethnic minority states has been the site of many ethnic wars. A military dictator rules the nation and refuses citizens' attempts to democratize the country. This military regime attempts to control every religious activity. Almost all Christian missions were expelled in 1966, but thankfully the seeds of evangelism had already taken root and Christians have since held fast through adversity. Pray that the church will help to build bridges between different ethnic groups.

NIGERIA

Since leaving the British Commonwealth in 1960, Nigeria has known only one decade of elected government. That may be changing with the February 1999 election of General Olusegun Obasanjo as President. Obasanjo, who says he committed his life to God while he served a political prison sentence, has many challenges in leading the nation and rebuilding the economy. Islam has often been given preferential treatment over Christianity. Northern Nigeria's predominately Muslim population has terrorized Christians and destroyed churches. The church in Nigeria is strong, but there is concern over the rise of foreign cults and the mixing of Christianity with the country's traditional fetish beliefs. Pray that the church will cling to biblical teaching and be a light to their nation.

NORTH KOREA

After World War II, Korea was partitioned and a Communist regime installed in the North. Today, it is one of the most repressive and isolated Communist regimes in the world. North Korea denies its citizens every kind of human rights. Thankfully, because of the flooding and famine that have swept this nation, North Korea's isolationist government has been forced to open its borders to humanitarian aid from foreign countries. Although Christians must practice their faith in deep secrecy and constant danger, they are adding to their numbers daily by reaching out to their relatives with the message of hope — Jesus Christ. Pray that God uses North Korea's famine to draw many to the Bread of Life.

OMAN

Oman has been an absolute monarchy since 1970 when Sultan Qaboos took control, declaring, "Oman in the past was in darkness...but a new dawn will rise." While Qaboos was able to increase the country's wealth, another darkness persists — the darkness in the hearts of Oman's people who are caught in the clutches of Islam. The Christian population consists almost entirely of foreign workers, with perhaps no more than twenty indigenous believers. Pray that the Christian foreigners will have opportunities to share Jesus Christ with the citizens of Oman.

PAKISTAN

Pakistan gained independence from Britain in 1947, but has been unstable ever since. Its people have suffered through three wars and endured military regimes and corrupt governments. Today, militant Islamic forces in Pakistan have initiated much violence against Christians. Many Pakistani Christians have been falsely accused of breaking Law 295C (blaspheming Mohammed) — a crime punishable by death. Some have even been killed by mobs after being acquitted of such charges. In 1998, a proposal was made to officially adopt Muslim Sharia law as the law of the land, which would bring about even more persecution. Despite hardships, Christians continue in love and perseverance, boldly sharing Jesus Christ. Pray that the Sharia law proposal is defeated in Pakistan's parliament.

QATAR

Almost all of Qatar is covered by desert, but there are huge oil reserves beneath the ground. The desolation of the countryside is mirrored in the hearts of Qatar's citizens. Before 1980, there were no known believers in Qatar. The emir and his family have declared the strict Wahabbi branch of Sunni Islam to be the state religion. Criticism of the Muslim faith or the ruling family is a crime. Women live under even harsher rules — they are not allowed to drive or travel abroad without permission from male relatives. Foreign believers may not worship publicly or even celebrate Jesus' birth. Christians must find creative ways to share their faith in Jesus Christ with the people of Qatar. Pray for the Lord to raise up an army of believers in Qatar.

SAUDI ARABIA

When Islam gained control of Saudi Arabia 1,300 years ago, all Christians were expelled. Believers are treated no better today. Christians have been arrested on false charges, imprisoned, and even beheaded because of their faith. Even foreign Christians visiting Saudi Arabia are not allowed to meet together and worship. Since 1992, more than 360 cases have been documented in which Christian expatriates were arrested for taking part in private worship. Saudi Arabia has signed many agreements over the years regarding religious freedom, such as U.N. and international human rights conventions, but these words have not been backed by actions. U.S. officials have approached the Saudi government about their pledges to practise religious tolerance to everyone, including Americans. Despite the threat of persecution, the followers of Jesus Christ press on, finding innovative ways to meet and encourage each other. Pray for strength for Christians in prison in Saudi Arabia.

SOMALIA

In 1969, dictator Siad Barre took control of Somalia, relying on Cold War politics to gain foreign aid and weapons. Barre also exploited clan warfare within Somalia to retain power. When Barre's government was toppled in 1991, Somalia could no longer be considered a single country, but a collection of fighting ethnic groups and clans. With no central government, the enforcement of strict Muslim law varies from area to area. Fellowship among believers is dangerous, since Muslim persecution is strong in many parts of the country. Many Christians have fled to neighbouring countries. But believers press on with the knowledge that Jesus will provide the comfort and fellowship they need. Pray that Christians continue to walk in those truths.

SRI LANKA

This fertile island with its palm-lined beaches and exotic tropical fruits is a potential paradise, but since the early 1980s violence has reigned in Sri Lanka. Civil war broke out in 1983 between two powerful political factions, and since then Sri Lanka has been in a near-continuous state of emergency. Many Sri Lankans have negative attitudes towards believers, perceiving Christianity as a foreign religion and a colonial imposition. Two centuries ago, Christianity had much influence in the country, but today believers are persecuted by the Buddhist majority and face restrictions on choice of profession and access to education. Pray that many in this war-scarred country will find peace in Jesus Christ.

SUDAN

Africa's largest country is experiencing an onslaught of persecution. The Muslim government of Khartoum in the North has declared a jihad, or holy war, against the mostly Christian South. Omar Hassan al-Turabi, an Islamic leader, has stated that anyone who opposes Islam "has no future." Muslim students are recruited out of universities and told that they can keep whatever they pillage if they join the war against non-Muslims. Since 1985, approximately two million have perished due to the genocide. Because of the war, famine has plagued the country as people are unable to plant and harvest. Families in the South are terrorized — fathers killed, mothers raped, and children sold into slavery. Yet in the midst of these atrocities, the body of Christ in Sudan remains strong, worshipping their Saviour and leading others to Him. Pray that Omar Hassan al-Turabi will come to a saving knowledge of Jesus Christ.

SYRIA

The president of Syria, Hafez al-Assad, gained power in a 1970 coup. In 1973, Syria was declared a secular state, but Muslims are still given preferential treatment in many areas of society. The Syrian government rules with an iron fist — the Emergency Law of 1963 allows authorities to conduct "preventative" arrests and hold detainees without legal safeguards. Christians find it difficult to spread the Gospel freely under such conditions. Missionaries are not given visas to enter the country, so Christians are able to exhibit their faith only in professional and informal friendship settings. Ask God to break the iron fist of the Syrian dictator.

TAJIKISTAN

Seventy years of Communist rule left this country in economic shambles. Since it gained independence from the Soviet Union in 1992, Tajikistan has suffered from corruption, civil war, and poverty. Many people struggle to find enough food each day. Life in this Muslim country is very harsh, and the influence of Islam is increasing greatly. Christians must carefully guard any evidence of their faith. Those who have any Gospel materials consider themselves fortunate. Pray for an abundance of Bibles and Christian training materials.

TIBET (Mainland China)

The people of Tibet live at some of the highest altitudes on earth. The vast majority of Tibetans are Buddhist. In 1950, Chinese Communists invaded and forced Tibet's political and religious leader, the Dalai Lama, to flee to India. The Communists soon stripped Tibet of its cultural and religious heritage. Today, Christians find themselves trapped between the oppression of Buddhism and the oppression of Communism. By one estimate, there may be as few as 300 believers in Tibet. Opposed by their government, their culture, and a false religion, Buddhists who convert to Christianity are forced to overcome many obstacles to grow in Christ. Pray that God will open the hearts of Tibetan Buddhists to His love.

TUNISIA

While Tunisia's government has declared Islam to be the state religion, fundamentalist Muslims are pressuring the government to make more concessions to their intolerant beliefs. The church in Tunisia is struggling at best. A century of missionary activity has produced little results in a land besieged by spiritual warfare. By one account there are less than fifty believers, and historically, most do not keep the faith for long in this oppressive environment. Christian literature is not openly distributed, and with so few believers dissemination would be difficult. Pray that the body of Christ will take root and multiply.

TURKEY

Turkey's Ottoman Empire was for centuries the guardian of the holy places of Islam. Today, the influence of the Muslim faith is rising. According to *Operation World*, Turkey is one of the most unreached nations in the world. Of its 55 million people, only a small per cent have heard the Gospel. For the few in Turkey who dare profess Jesus Christ, life can be dangerous. In January 1998, the St. Therapon Greek Orthodox church in Istanbul was plundered and set on fire. The body of the 73-year-old caretaker of the church was found, with hands bound and skull caved in, at the bottom of the church's well. Evangelizing is difficult because Turks tend to place Christians in the same category as Armenian terrorists and Jehovah's Witnesses. In March 1998, top generals in Turkey's military urged government efforts to curb the influence of Islam on the secular government, maintaining Turkey as a non-Islamic state. Pray that the government remains non-Islamic, and for strength for Christians in Turkey facing intense persecution.

TURKMENISTAN

Despite the collapse of the Communist government of the Soviet Union in 1990 and Turkmenistan's subsequent freedom in 1991, many remnants of the old system remain. Soon after Turkmenistan gained its freedom, President Saparmurad Niyazov named himself Turkmenbashi, or head of the Turkmen, and built a cult around himself. Anyone who attempts to run against him in "democratic" elections is subjected to harassment. Turkmenistan is also slowly proceeding toward Islamization. As a result, Christianity in Turkmenistan has suffered greatly. One church in the capital city of Ashkebad, which had grown to over 100 members, was forced to close in 1997 due to a new law restricting Christian worship. Christian university students have been threatened with expulsion. Yet believers, although few in number, are influencing their society. Through the *Jesus* film, which has been well received, many are being exposed to the saving grace of Jesus Christ. Pray for souls to be won into the kingdom through these efforts.

UNITED ARAB EMIRATES

In 1971, the Trucial states in the lower Persian Gulf changed from a British protectorate to a loose confederation of sheikdoms called the United Arab Emirates. Today, this oil-rich nation claims Sunni Islam as the official religion. Only foreign Christians have freedom to worship and witness. Christian education and witnessing to nationals are severely restricted. However, several Christian medical agencies are allowed to operate, showing the love of Jesus Christ to the people of the U.A.E. through selfless service. Pray that the government will lift restrictions on Christian nationals.

UZBEKISTAN

During the Cold War, Christians in Uzbekistan suffered under the totalitarian regime of Communism. A period of relative freedom followed the fall of the Soviet Union, but today Christians in Uzbekistan are again experiencing difficulties. Each church must have an official government registration in order to hold services. Police have made unannounced visits to churches, demanding to see their registration papers. Churches that cannot immediately produce their registration are closed and their doors sealed by the police. Pastors have been arrested and detained, and members threatened. Many Christians in Uzbekistan continue to worship and reach out to others, despite government threats. Pray for discipleship and training for Uzbekistan's believers, that they may grow strong in the Lord. Pray that the church continues to be a light to those in darkness.

VIETNAM

Vietnam, ruled by France until 1954, has historically been a hotbed of struggle. The Communists had a foothold in North Vietnam and took over all of Vietnam in 1975. At this point, many Christians fled, but those who remained have not allowed persecution to stop them from following Jesus. Believers are harassed, beaten, and imprisoned for illegally preaching or organizing evangelistic activities. Instead of being weakened by persecution, the faith of Vietnamese Christians is growing and the body of Christ is becoming stronger. Pray for the Hmong and other tribes that are prohibited from having Bibles in their own languages.

YEMEN

The great cities of the Queen of Sheba, who traded gifts with King Solomon, are buried beneath Yemen's desert sands. Yemen had many Christians until the seventh century, when Muslims overran the country and cut off nearly all outside influences. Yemen was two states until 1990, and today tensions between the North and South threaten this country's very existence. Yemen is one of the world's least evangelized countries, and the government will not allow the few resident Christians to witness. Their walk is difficult due to discouragement and isolation from the rest of the body of Christ, yet some Christian expatriates are working and quietly witnessing for Jesus in Yemen. Pray that believers will be strengthened and encouraged daily, and that Yemen nationals will be won for Christ.

COUNTRY SUMMARY INFORMATION FROM THE VOICE OF THE MARTYRS NEWSLETTERS AND REPORTS, OPERATION WORLD, FREEDOM IN THE WORLD: 1996-97, AND COMPASS DIRECT.

What Can I Do?

You Can Pray...

Look over the country descriptions in this book and choose a country to pray for during the week. Pray for the specific needs of that country, for the protection of the believers there, for new hearts to be won to the Gospel, and that the persecutors in that country would come to know the love of Jesus Christ.

- Pray that the Holy Spirit would give you special things and people to pray for in that country — be as specific as possible.

- As you go through your day be aware of that country — find it on a globe, look it up in the library or on the Internet (The Voice of the Martyrs web site is www.persecution.com), and watch for it on the news. Look up scriptures in the Bible to pray over that country.

- Share prayer requests for that country with your Bible study, Sunday school class, or friends. Form a prayer group to meet and pray on a regular basis for different countries.

- Create a bulletin board in your church or youth group area where you and your friends can post the answers to your prayers.

- Say a short prayer whenever you think of that country throughout the week. At the end of the week ask God if He wants you to continue to pray for that country or to choose another to pray for.

You Can Identify...

Hundreds of thousands of Christians risk their lives by gathering to worship Jesus every week. We in America may never know the extent of such repression. Hold a mock underground church meeting in a home or at your church. Give each participant a password or secret knock that they will need in order to enter your meeting. You could even hold your meeting outside in the woods. Then have people who are dressed as police invade your meeting. Have only one or two Bibles to share in the group. Use only the light from a lantern or candle.

You Can Share the Gospel...

Discuss with your youth group the idea of reaching out to countries that persecute Christians. Educate yourself on different cultures and the best way to reach them for Jesus. Find out about and support missionaries to those countries and pray for them regularly. Find out what their needs are and see how you can help them be met, whether it is obtaining Bibles in their language, supplying food, or supporting them financially.

You Can Dramatize...

Create a short sketch or a series of sketches to be performed before your church congregation or youth group from the stories in this book or martyrs you have researched yourself. Select martyrs from both the past and present. Put on your plays and then invite people to join prayer groups or pray weekly as described above.

You Can Write...

To your elected officials. Write a letter to or e-mail your elected officials in Washington and in your state capital. Inform them of specific human rights violations committed against Christians in various countries around the world. Let them know that you are also passing this information on to several of your friends. Request that they investigate these violations and propose sanctions against the governments of these countries until these violations end. Their addresses can be found in the blue pages in your phone book or call the reference desk at your local library.

To the ambassador. You can be a voice on behalf of your persecuted brothers and sisters in specific countries. Write the ambassador from that foreign government or the United States ambassador to that country communicating your concern over the treatment of Christians in his country. Politely protest the continued attacks on Christians citing any specific incidents of which you know. Addresses can be obtained from your local library, the United Nations web site: www.un.org, or at www.embassyworld.com.

To the officials of foreign governments. The Religious Prisoners Congressional Task Force (www.house.gov/pitts) encourages American citizens to directly appeal to foreign governments on behalf of specific religious prisoners. You can find other information on doing this at www.persecution.com under "Ministry Opportunities" or at www.jesusfreaks.net.

To the editor of your local newspaper. Educate your community on the horrors faced by Christians worldwide. Make sure you call the newspaper's editorial staff and ask for their letter writing guidelines. Many have a maximum word count and abiding by that will give your letter a better chance of being printed.

To your friends. E-mail spreads information very quickly. Create an e-mail distribution list that has the addresses of several friends and forward them information about the atrocities happening to Christians around the world. By keeping them informed, they can be praying for these individuals and can be writing letters or sending e-mails of their own to elected officials, foreign governments, or other friends.

Your voice will make a difference!

You Can Become a Partner in Serving the Persecuted Church...

You can write, call, or e-mail The Voice of the Martyrs at:

The Voice of the Martyrs
P.O. Box 443
Bartlesville, OK 74005
(800) 747-0085
e-mail address: thevoice@vom-usa.org

Sign up for their monthly newsletter. Visit their web site (www.persecution.com) frequently to get new prayer requests and updates. Find out other ways you can help in their ministry to the persecuted church.

Request VOM's Voice Packet of their Special Issue newsletters which contain country updates and a prayer poster for your wall. A letter with suggestions on how to share these with your friends is also included. Distribute these and urge your friends to pray and support organizations that minister to the persecuted church.

Endnotes

Strengthened by Angels (pp. 30-36)

Grant, Myrna. *Vanya* (Lake Mary, FL: Creation House, 1974, pp. 50-60, 155-156, 164, 171). Used by permission.

Cuban Prisoner Quote (p. 49)

Wurmbrand, Richard. *In the Face of Surrender: Over 200 Challenging and Inspiring Stories of Overcomers* (New Brunswick, NJ: Bridge-Logos Publishers, 1998, p. 138).

"Employ Your Whole Power Upon Me!" (p. 60)

Lockyer, Herbert. *Last Words of Saints and Sinners* (Grand Rapids, MI: Kregel Publications, 1969, p. 149).

"I Will Go Straight to God"/Afraid? Of What? (pp. 74-75)

Hefley, James and Marti. *By Their Blood: Christian Martyrs of the Twentieth Century* (Grand Rapids, MI: Baker Books, 1996, p. 57).

"My Life is a Prayer" (pp. 80-81)

Wurmbrand, Richard. *In the Face of Surrender: Over 200 Challenging and Inspiring Stories of Overcomers* (New Brunswick, NJ: Bridge-Logos Publishers, 1998, pp. 219-220).

Why I Came (p. 83)

Lockyer, Herbert. *Last Words of Saints and Sinners* (Grand Rapids, MI: Kregel Publications, 1969, p. 140).

"There Is Freedom Everywhere" (p. 100)

Wurmbrand, Richard. *Tortured for Christ* (Bartlesville, OK: Living Sacrifice Book Company, 1967, pp. 138-140).

Making a Better World (pp. 115-116)

Wurmbrand, Richard. *In God's Underground* (Bartlesville, OK: Living Sacrifice Book Company, 1968, pp. 60-63).

Siberian Prisoner Prayer (p. 117)

Wurmbrand, Richard. *In the Face of Surrender: Over 200 Challenging and Inspiring Stories of Overcomers* (New Brunswick, NJ: Bridge-Logos Publishers, 1998, p. 23).

Geleazium Quote (p. 135)

Lockyer, Herbert. *Last Words of Saints and Sinners* (Grand Rapids, MI: Kregel Publications, 1969, p. 145).

"I Rest in the Arms of God" (p. 141)

Wurmbrand, Richard. *In the Face of Surrender: Over 200 Challenging and Inspiring Stories of Overcomers* (New Brunswick, NJ: Bridge-Logos Publishers, 1998, pp. 184-185).

Andronicus Quote (p. 141)

Lockyer, Herbert. *Last Words of Saints and Sinners* (Grand Rapids, MI: Kregel Publications, 1969, pp. 139-40).

Robert Jaffray Quote (p. 152)

Lockyer, Herbert. *Last Words of Saints and Sinners* (Grand Rapids, MI: Kregel Publications, 1969, p. 154).

Gospels Flames (pp. 160-161)

Wurmbrand, Richard. *In the Face of Surrender: Over 200 Challenging and Inspiring Stories of Overcomers* (New Brunswick, NJ: Bridge-Logos Publishers, 1998, p. 234).

Felicitas Quote (p. 169)

Chenu, Bruno, et al. *The Book of Christian Martyrs* (New York: The Crossroads Publishing Company, 1990, p. 70).

John Peary Quote (p. 180)

Lockyer, Herbert. *Last Words of Saints and Sinners* (Grand Rapids, MI: Kregel Publications, 1969, p. 148).

Prisoner Quote (p. 185)

Wurmbrand, Richard. *In the Face of Surrender: Over 200 Challenging and Inspiring Stories of Overcomers* (New Brunswick, NJ: Bridge-Logos Publishers, 1998, pp. 21-22).

Girolamo Savanarola Quote (p. 223)

Lockyer, Herbert. *Last Words of Saints and Sinners* (Grand Rapids, MI: Kregel Publications, 1969, pp. 150-151).

The Happiest Day (p. 224)

Wurmbrand, Richard. *In the Face of Surrender: Over 200 Challenging and Inspiring Stories of Overcomers* (New Brunswick, NJ: Bridge-Logos Publishers, 1998, p. 177).

"I Am God" (p. 235)

Wurmbrand, Richard. *Tortured for Christ* (Bartlesville, OK: Living Sacrifice Book Company, 1967, p. 42).

Richard Wurmbrand Quote (p. 257)

Wurmbrand, Richard. *In the Face of Surrender: Over 200 Challenging and Inspiring Stories of Overcomers* (New Brunswick, NJ: Bridge-Logos Publishers, 1998, p. 21).

"If You Love Jesus, Don't Sing" (pp. 258-262)

White, Tom. *God's Missiles over Cuba* (Bartlesville, OK: Living Sacrifice Book Company, 1981, pp. 102-111).

Two Chinese Prisoners Quote (p. 266)

Wurmbrand, Richard. *In the Face of Surrender: Over 200 Challenging and Inspiring Stories of Overcomers* (New Brunswick, NJ: Bridge-Logos Publishers, 1998, p. 224).

A Temporary, Light Affliction (pp. 271-272)

Wurmbrand, Richard. *In the Face of Surrender: Over 200 Challenging and Inspiring Stories of Overcomers* (New Brunswick, NJ: Bridge-Logos Publishers, 1998, pp. 225-226).

Chinese Christian's Quote (p. 280)

Wurmbrand, Richard. *In the Face of Surrender: Over 200 Challenging and Inspiring Stories of Overcomers* (New Brunswick, NJ: Bridge-Logos Publishers, 1998, p. 185).

"It Is Life that I Love" (pp. 283-284)

Chenu, Bruno, et al. *The Book of Christian Martyrs* (New York: The Crossroads Publishing Company, 1990, pp. 57-58).

The Courage of a Child (p. 288)

Wurmbrand, Richard. *In the Face of Surrender: Over 200 Challenging and Inspiring Stories of Overcomers* (New Brunswick, NJ: Bridge-Logos Publishers, 1998, p. 194).

"Note Well Our Faces" (pp. 298-303)

Chenu, Bruno, et al. *The Book of Christian Martyrs* (New York: The Crossroads Publishing Company, 1990, pp. 61-62).

Commanded to Preach (p. 305)

Wurmbrand, Richard. *In the Face of Surrender: Over 200 Challenging and Inspiring Stories of Overcomers* (New Brunswick, NJ: Bridge-Logos Publishers, 1998, pp. 140-141).

Where Do I Find Out More About Martyrs?

Where we got our information...

Chenu, Bruno, et al. *The Book of Christian Martyrs*. Translated by John Bowden. New York: The Crossroads Publishing Company, 1990.

Christian History: Dietrich Bonhoeffer. Vol. X, no. 4 (1991).

Christian History: John Bunyan. Vol. V, no. 3 (1986).

Grant, Myrna. *Vanya*. Lake Mary, FL: Creation House, 1974.

Hefley, James and Marti. *By Their Blood: Christian Martyrs of the Twentieth Century*. Second edition. Grand Rapids, MI: Baker Books, 1996.

Faith Under Fire, produced and directed by Stephen Yake, 30 minutes, The Voice of the Martyrs, 1998, videocassette.

The Faithful, produced and directed by Stephen Yake, 15 minutes, Steve Green Ministries and The Voice of the Martyrs, 1998, videocassette.

Foxe, John. *Foxe's Book of Martyrs*. Belfast: Ambassador Productions, 1995.

Foxe, John. *Foxe's Book of Martyrs*. Prepared by W. Grinton Berry. Grand Rapids, MI: Baker Book House, twenty-first printing 1998.

Johnstone, Patrick. *Operation World: A Day-by Day Guide to Praying for the World*. Carlisle: OM Publishing, 1993.

Lockyer, Herbert. *Last Words of Saints and Sinners*. Grand Rapids, MI: Kregel Publications, 1969.

Tortured for Christ, 30 minutes, Department of Mission to Europe's Millions, Inc., 1967, videocassette.

The Voice of the Martyrs monthly newsletters (formerly known as *Jesus to the Communist World*). Issues ranging from 1968 to 1999.

Van Braght, Thieleman J. *Martyrs Mirror*. Translated by Joseph F. Sohm. Scottsdale, PA: Herald Press, 1660.

White, Tom. *God's Missiles Over Cuba*. Bartlesville, OK: Living Sacrifice Book Company, 1981.

Wurmbrand, Richard. *In God's Underground*. Edited by Charles Foley. Bartlesville, OK: Living Sacrifice Book Company, 1968.

Wurmbrand, Richard. *In the Face of Surrender: Over 200 Challenging and Inspiring Stories of Overcomers*. New Brunswick, NJ: Bridge-Logos Publishers, 1998.

Wurmbrand, Richard. *Tortured for Christ*. Bartlesville, OK: Living Sacrifice Book Company, 1967.

Other Suggested Titles...

Anderson, Ken, *Bold as a Lamb: Pastor Samuel Lamb and the Underground Church of China*. Grand Rapids, MI: Zondervan Publishing House, 1991.

Between Two Tigers. Compiled by Tom White. Bartlesville, OK: Living Sacrifice Book Company, 1996.

Edwards, Brian, *God's Outlaw: The Story of William Tyndale and the English Bible*. Darlington: Evangelical Press, 1976.

Foxe, John. *The New Foxe's Book of Martyrs*. Rewritten and updated by Harold J. Chadwick. New Brunswick, NJ: Bridge-Logos Publishers, 1997.

Hanks, Geoffrey. *70 Great Christians: Changing the World*. Fearn, Scotland: Christian Focus Publications Ltd., 1992.

Sheikh, Bliquis. *I Dared to Call Him Father*. With Richard H. Schneider. Eastbourne: Kingsway, STL, 1979.

Whalin, W. Terry, et al. *One Bright Shining Path: Faith in the Midst of Terrorism*. Wheaton, IL: Crossway Books, 1993.

Wurmbrand, Richard. *From Torture to Triumph!* London: Donasch, 1991.

Wurmbrand, Sabina. *The Pastor's Wife*. Bartlesville, OK: Living Sacrifice Book Company, 1970.

Alphabetical Index

Chronological Index

About dc Talk

Toby McKeehan   Michael Tait   Kevin Max

Since releasing their album *Jesus Freak*, dc Talk has emerged as a leader in the pursuit of melding rock 'n' roll with provocative questions of faith.

Although various rock predecessors have examined spiritual issues — U2, Van Morrison, and Bob Dylan immediately come to mind — dc Talk has taken the notion to new lengths, both in commercial terms and depth of artistic exploration. Numerous Dove Awards, three Grammy Awards, two platinum albums, one gold album, and two gold-certified long-form videos attest to the group's ability to bridge the gap between religious and secular audiences.

"We are very open about our Christian faith," says Toby McKeehan, "but when we make our records we want to create a musical experience that anyone can immerse themselves in. One of our goals is to encourage listeners to question themselves and to seek out truth."

Authoring the book *Jesus Freaks* is the newest venture in an ongoing growth process which began when the three members first met in the mid-1980s while attending college in Virginia. After relocating to Nashville, dc Talk released a series of increasingly ambitious — and successful — albums, beginning with their self-titled 1989 debut; followed by their gold-certified 1990 sophomore album *Nu Thang*; the platinum-certified 1992 opus *Free at Last*; 1995's *Jesus Freak*, a platinum-plus watershed which afforded the group more mainstream success than ever before; and 1998's *Supernatural*, which reflects the maturity and sophistication of their latest stage of development and growth.

In addition to their recordings, live performance is a crucial part of the dc Talk story, and the group's fiery onstage delivery has earned respect from virtually all quarters.

"When you yourself are having as much fun — if not more — than the audience, that's the essence of a live show," says Michael Tait.

Now, with *Jesus Freaks*, their first book, they launch into a new media form to challenge readers to question their standards of faith and dedication. By giving these stories a platform from which to be heard, they hope to impact the world in a way they never have before.

Whether forging strong bonds with concert audiences, expressing their faith in the recording studio, or confronting readers with no-compromise stories of commitment, dc Talk strives to treat their audiences as equals rather than receptors. McKeehan says, "We want to create art that encourages people to think about the things we think about — spiritual issues and truth." Max adds, "Just as we all share the idea of caring and conscience, we also share the hunger to find truth and meaning in life."

With *Jesus Freaks*, dc Talk once again encourages each of us to set out on our own journey to discover our response to the Gospel of Jesus Christ.

LIVE LIKE A JESUS FREAK

dc Talk

Being a Jesus Freak is all about following Jesus.
He never promised it would be easy. Quite the opposite.
Look at his words:

*"If anyone would come after me, He must deny himself and take
up his cross and follow me. For whoever wants to save his life will
lose it, but whoever loses his life for me will find it"*
MATTHEW 16:24-25

This book's combination of real life stories, challenging essays,
ideas for reaching out to those persecuted anywhere in the world,
contact information, discussion-generating questions and much
more will help you to . . .

Live Like a Jesus Freak

0 86347 501 9
Eagle Publishing Ltd

PROMISES FOR A JESUS FREAK

dc Talk

With the enormous popularity of dc Talk's *Jesus Freaks* comes a pocket sized edition that builds on its original ideas.

Promises for a Jesus Freak's pocket sized format has been designed with both 'take it everywhere' and 'give it away' potential! The idea is that anyone who has read *Jesus Freaks* and has been inspired by the stories of men and women of faith through the ages will be able to use *Promises for a Jesus Freak* to look up Bible verses that speak to the difficult life issues they face today. Life changing scriptures in an accessible format can be one of the best ways to both create and satisfy a hunger for God's word.

As with the other titles in the *Jesus Freaks* series, this book uses striking graphic design and images to create a unique product.

0 86347 467 5
Eagle Publishing Ltd

JESUS FREAKS JOURNAL

dc Talk

Journal writing has long been considered a valuable tool for self discovery and spiritual growth. It is also an excellent tool for developing writing and thinking skills as well as an opportunity to reason through new ideas and reflect on lessons learned. A journal gives us a place to look back and see how we've grown, to remember what God has done for us in the past and renew our goals and visions for the future.

Beyond being a great looking cased book, this Jesus Freaks Journal is another way for people to become radical in their faith. To those who enjoy writing there is ample space to record their deepest thoughts, fears, hopes, joys and aspiration. For first-time journal writers, there are prompts and suggestions throughout the book to provide a way to get started on this spiritual discipline.

Presented in the same eye-catching style as the best selling *Jesus Freaks* this is an essential aid for anyone concerned with the suffering world-wide church.

0 86347 502 7
Eagle Publishing Ltd

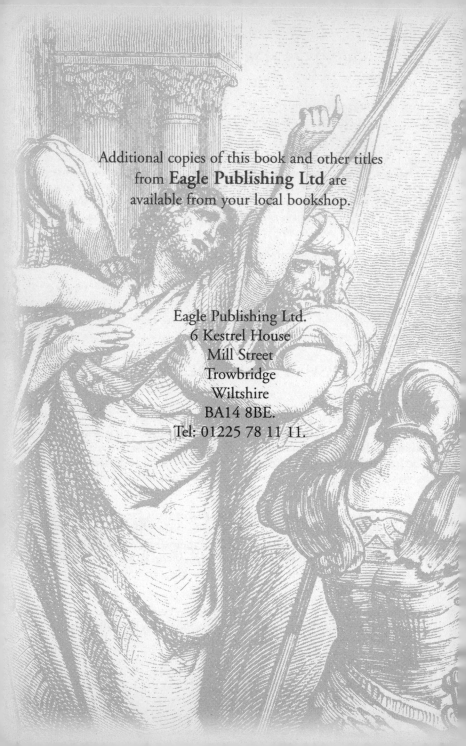

Additional copies of this book and other titles
from **Eagle Publishing Ltd** are
available from your local bookshop.

Eagle Publishing Ltd.
6 Kestrel House
Mill Street
Trowbridge
Wiltshire
BA14 8BE.
Tel: 01225 78 11 11.